THE OFFICIAL

# Unicorn
# SPiT®

USER'S
HANDBOOK

Let Your Creative Juices Flow With Over 50 Colorful Projects for Home Decor, Apparel, Artwork, and Much More!

## MICHELLE NICOLE

# The Official Unicorn SPiT® User's Handbook:

Let Your Creative Juices Flow With Over 50 Colorful Projects
for Home Decor, Apparel, Artwork, and Much More!

## Michelle Nicole

Editor: Kelly Reed
Project manager: Lisa Brazieal
Marketing coordinator: Mercedes Murray
Copyeditor: Michelle Drown
Proofreader: Patricia J. Pane
Interior design: Aren Straiger
Interior layout: Kim Scott/Bumpy Design
Cover production: Aren Straiger
Cover Images: Amanda Fritz
Co-author: Lisa Kanarek

ISBN: 978-1-68198-719-4
1st Edition (1st printing, August 2021)
© 2021 Michelle Nicole
All photographs © Amanda Fritz unless otherwise noted.

Rocky Nook Inc.
1010 B Street, Suite 350
San Rafael, CA 94901
USA

www.rockynook.com

Distributed in the U.K. and Europe by Publishers Group U.K.
Distributed in the U.S. and all other territories by Ingram Publisher Services

Library of Congress Control Number: 2020949321

This book is printed on acid-free paper.
Printed in Korea

# Dedication

This book is dedicated to my Mom and Dad, Darlene and Nick, and my childhood home in New Mexico, Moon Ranch.

In the desolate Chihuahuan Desert, at the base of the Franklin Mountains, sits Moon Ranch. The elaborate, sprawling, A-frame rock home has a single-wide trailer for a heart. As a family, we treasure-hunted in the arroyos of the back desert. Dumped furnishings, driftwood, and fossils became creative materials for building our home and creating art. It became a beacon of light—folks and animals in need always found their way to our doorstep.

Here, mom taught me how to create, heal, and cook. Her folklore stories, playing in the desert, and the colors that surrounded me trained me to be a great mom and artist. Dad showed me how to imagine—and realize—big visions, to try without fear of failing, and to realize that failing allowed me to create new inventions.

I can build, cook, nurture animals and people. I take pride in a hard day's work, and sharing how to make beautiful things, all with joy and God in my heart.

You gave all of us kids a wonderful childhood. We are all so lucky to have you as our parents. God truly blessed us. You and that A-frame with a trailer in its heart will forever power mine.

Your Little Ding Bat,
Michelle Nicole

# Contents

# Introduction

## What is Unicorn SPiT?

Unicorn SPiT is a concentrated gel pigment that I often refer to as a shapeshifter. I created a groundbreaking formula to help people create art despite any physical, mental, or financial limitations. With Unicorn SPiT, you can dabble with many varieties of art without going broke buying endless amounts of supplies.

Unicorn SPiT can be anything the experimental artist would like it to be: paint, wood stain, wood dye, fabric dye, fabric paint/ink, glass colorant, faux finish, or watercolor. It can even be used in place of oil and acrylic paints. These vibrant, non-toxic, low-VOC products are aromatherapy infused. One of my favorite aspects of SPiT is that it can be applied with a brush, foam pad, spray bottle, airbrush, cloth, paper towel, or even your gloved hands. Because the product doesn't contain microplastics or harsh chemicals, you can allow Unicorn SPiT to dry on your brushes, paint palettes, and stencils without damaging them.

And it's easy to correct mistakes by simply wiping them away with a damp cloth. Even after it's dry!

My first version of Unicorn SPiT was watery. My sheer laziness inspired me to make the formula more concentrated and thicker because I didn't want my customers running out too fast; I couldn't handle all of the shipping requests. So, I created a new concentrated version and Unicorn SPiT evolved from a wood stain to a concentrated gel stain and glaze, all in one. My customers quickly discovered that this new formula could be used in ways other than just staining wood.

## How I Created Unicorn SPiT

When I created Unicorn SPiT in 2015, I never imagined my colorful concoction would go from being created in a spaghetti pot in my kitchen to being sold at major art and hobby stores around the world. What most people don't know is I created the product out of necessity.

When I was 21, I moved to Kansas City, Kansas, to live with my older brother, Tony, who operated an adult day-care center there. The center was a place for elderly and disabled adults to spend the day with others. I loved spending my days with the folks, but soon noticed how bored some of them were. So, I introduced arts and crafts days. We started with typical projects: macaroni pictures and hook rugs. The ladies participated, but the men weren't interested.

One day after work I found a desk on the side of the road, loaded it into my car, and took it to the senior center. It didn't take long for the men to get down to work. They sanded the desk and made it look new. But it was bare wood and I'm all about color—lots of it. However, the folks refused to apply paint to real wood.

We brainstormed ways to add color to the desk that didn't include paint. We tried beet juice and powdered juice mix. Our mixture brightened both the desk and the men's spirits. They were excited to add color to more projects. The women got involved too and soon almost everyone was adding color to the roadside finds I brought into the center. Even people who had previously spent their days in the corner staring at the walls began to participate.

## One of My Inspirations

One man, Johnny B., stood out from the others. He had severe multiple sclerosis and couldn't hold a paintbrush. I taped paint brushes to his hands, but that didn't work. Then I discovered he could use the side of his hand to manipulate the stains into fun patterns.

Realizing that Johnny—and other residents—were going to use their hands to color the furniture, I decided to develop a non-toxic product that didn't emit harmful fumes or irritate the skin. After much trial and error, I developed a vibrantly colorful stain that worked, was safe to use, and smelled like jasmine.

## My Future Was Unsure

After budget cuts forced the center to shut down, I thought about going back to my previous job at the bank, but day-care costs for my two sons would have wiped out what I earned. Instead, I started a custom refinishing business. I followed the trash routes during bulk pickup weeks and found items I could take home, refinish, and sell. People loved my finished pieces—it was the first time many of them had seen colorfully stained furniture. Social media

embraced my unique, colorful style. I made just enough money to make ends meet, but not enough to make my mortgage payment. I was going to have to sell my house.

When my life was at its worst, I met—and eventually married—Don. I continued refurbishing old furniture in my signature style and soon people were asking to buy the stain I had created. I took a leap of faith and sold everything I owned—my clothes, pots and pans, silverware, even my vehicle. The only things I kept were my grandmother's dining room table set and my kids' possessions. With that seed money, I was able to buy enough ingredients to make my first bulk batch of SPiT for selling.

## A Business is Born

I sold Unicorn SPiT in mason jars that I mailed to buyers around the country. Unfortunately, many of them would break en route. I had to figure out a better way to get my product to my customers. I called my brother, Tony, who had moved to Arizona by then, and asked him for help as I was out of money.

"Your idea is never going to work," he told me when I asked him to fund my business, "but I'll lend you the money." He shopped around and found the ingredients and shatterproof bottles at lower prices. Then he said, "If this ever takes off, I'll be your 50-percent partner." We're still partners today.

After ordering the new supplies, I started a Facebook group for customers to share the ways in which they were using Unicorn SPiT. Based on their feedback, I created new colors and made the product into a concentrate so customers wouldn't have to order it as often, as filling orders became overwhelming. As the number of orders grew, I went from making Unicorn SPiT in spaghetti pots in my kitchen to using turkey fryers in my garage. I needed help, so I hired one of the drivers from the senior day-care center where I had worked. He helped me brew and bottle my product; my kids put the labels on the jars and cleaned the pots.

One day, I received an email from a major arts and crafts retail chain asking if I would send samples of my product for them to try and possibly carry in their stores. I put together a beautiful package containing each Unicorn SPiT color and sent it off. A month later, I still hadn't received a response from the retailer. Disappointed, I decided to refurbish my grandmother's kitchen table. I stripped it and used a product an epoxy company had sent me, which ruined my whole design. I stripped the table of the epoxy. During that time, I happened upon FAMOWOOD Glaze Coat at a local woodworking store and tried it on my grandma's table. It was amazing!

## The Evolution of Unicorn SPiT

At this point, my business had outgrown my garage and I was now renting an industrial bay—I had traded in my turkey fryers for 55-gallon drums and hired four more employees to handle orders. We were a proper cottage industry.

I sent an email to Eclectic Products LLC, the maker of FAMOWOOD Glaze Coat telling them how much I loved their product and asked if they would sponsor me so I could continue to make my art, as well as support their brand. They agreed and called me within 24 hours to set up a meeting.

I met with representatives from Eclectic, and they offered me a wonderful licensing agreement. As much as I was sad to let go of my manufacturing employees, I was thrilled to no longer have to operate the mortar mixer. One of the issues with handmaking Unicorn SPiT was that each batch was slightly different. When Eclectic Products took over manufacturing, sales, marketing, and shipping, I finally had a consistent product to offer my clients. Eclectic formulated Unicorn Spit into a consistent, high-quality, non-toxic, low VOC (Volatile Organic Compound) product and made it available worldwide.

There was another benefit to licensing my product to Eclectic. After being engaged for four years, I finally had time to plan my wedding to Don.

With my free time, I was able to develop new color concepts such as SPARKLiNG stain. I began experimenting with metallics and created a fantastic metallic stain product that my brother perfected. We're still working on the colors and making the prototypes available to my focus group for feedback.

Today, I continue to explore new ideas, like Unicorn SPiT METALLiCS—a product for artists perfected by artists.

## The Story Behind the Name

One of the questions I'm often asked is how I came up with the name Unicorn SPiT. I was refinishing furniture in my garage with help from my son, Johnny—staying busy was a good way to manage his ADHD. A woman brought us a mid-century modern desk that she wanted restored with a brown finish. Johnny and I sanded the desk and bought a brown stain. I was ready to color the piece when Don (at the time, my boyfriend) came home. He used to chew tobacco; he set his spit bottle down on the table and walked inside the house. Johnny accidentally knocked over the bottle, its contents spilling all over the freshly sanded piece of furniture. His face froze. "I'm going to die!" he said. I was upset, but as I wiped up the liquid with paper towels, I realized how pretty the color was. I told Johnny it was okay and asked him to grab the other spit jar from Don's truck so we could finish staining the piece.

Johnny couldn't believe we were coloring the desk with spit. He said, "If unicorns could spit, they would spit a rainbow. Instead of calling the stuff you make Unicorn Stain, you should call it Unicorn Spit." The name stuck. I considered changing it a few times, but ultimately, I wanted to celebrate our happy little accident.

## Why is There a lowercase "i" in the Name?

The lowercase "i" represents all the individual artists who are trying to stand out in a world overrun with mass-produced commercial merchandise. We are unique because each item we make is one-of-a-kind.

We are moms, dads, grandmothers, grandfathers, daughters, and sons: real people who are important to our community. There's no limit to where we can create, whether we're in a studio or a kitchen. We are local crafters, artists, carpenters, and family-owned business people. Unicorn SPiT is for anyone who wants to release their inner artist and shine—regardless of age, ability, or disability—in a market of corporate imitations.

We call the people who use Unicorn SPiT, "SPiT-TERS." After reading this book, you may find yourself going to thrift stores, yard sales, or garage sales in search of items to refinish. Don't be surprised if, when you spot the perfect piece, you say to yourself, "I can SPiT that!"

## Why Unicorn SPiT is Scented

While I was working at the adult day-care center, I began learning about aromatherapy. One of the folks at the center had Alzheimer's disease, which made him physically combative and always in a bad mood. I learned that jasmine was calming and so, one night, I took a vial of jasmine and put it into all of the colors I was mixing. The next morning, I brought the scented colors along with a diffuser and laid out the colors in front of the man on a board then covered in plastic. Within minutes, he began rubbing the colors around under the plastic. Each time he finished, I replaced the paper, and he moved the colors around again. He commented that his mother had a plant that smelled the same. Usually, he wandered off, but while working with the scented SPiT, he stayed put. He also became happy while he was creating art.

### Benefits of Jasmine in Original Unicorn SPiT

Jasmine will make you feel calm, relaxed, and content. The wonderful thing about using Unicorn SPiT is the smell; it is light and not overpowering. The oils absorb into your piece and helps deodorize it. Over time, when wood expands and contracts in response to the weather, don't be surprised if you get a little hint of jasmine for years to come.

### Benefits of Lemongrass in SPARKLiNG Unicorn SPiT

Lemongrass has the same stress-relieving benefits as jasmine, but it also makes me feel energetic. After smelling lemongrass, I feel alert, excited, and adventurous.

### Adding a Scent to the METALLiCS

Currently, I'm experimenting with new scents and one I'm really enjoying is teakwood. This scent makes me think of rich mahogany and leather-bound books. It gives me a feeling of strength, courage, and endurance.

## Therapeutic Benefits of Unicorn SPiT

Remember Johnny B.? He was one of my favorite folks at the senior day-care center. Before he started painting with Unicorn SPiT he worked with a physical therapist. Once a month, Johnny used a handcycle to increase his range of motion, but it didn't seem to help. The physical therapist tried other types of exercises too, but nothing worked.

I thought he might enjoy SPiTTiNG. I taped paint-brushes to his hand, but it didn't work so I tried a different idea. I put a wood board on the table, put Unicorn SPiT colors on top with water, and covered the board with plastic. Then I sprayed Johnny's hands with water and he moved his arms from side to side, smearing the paint around. There was no resistance as he worked to spread the colors from edge to edge. And he didn't get anything on his hands. He began doing the designs on the furniture tops.

The next time the physical therapist visited the center, he was shocked. He watched Johnny use a wide range of motion to move the colors where he desired. He could finally move his arms with a greater range!

I often hear from people in adult and child day-care centers, and those living with family or others who have physical challenges. They share their stories of how the motion of using Unicorn SPiT is a form of physical and sensory therapy for them. The colors spark something in them. The outreach of love from those touched by Unicorn SPiT inspires me every day. I read each email and letter and reply to them as I can.

## There's Only One Original Unicorn SPiT

Over the years, a handful of companies have tried to replicate Unicorn SPiT, but one thing they can't replicate is its authenticity, originality, and the devotion with which it is created. I developed Unicorn SPiT out of love, not greed. This is my passion. And the concentrated stains are now used and loved by people around the world. From an arts and crafts project inspired by working with the elderly and disabled, to a thriving global business—thanks to Eclectic Products—Unicorn SPiT is a family of loving, caring people who enjoy helping others. The mission for Unicorn SPiT remains the same: hope, creativity, and healing.

## What This Book Will Cover

Are you ready to find a piece of you that you've felt has always been missing? Are you ready to start feeling the benefits of exploring multiple art styles? Are you ready to allow your mind to communicate non-verbally and to activate your body and your senses of touch, hearing, and smell?

In this book, I'm going to show you how to express yourself through many forms of art. A few of my "SPiT FAMiLY" are going to share their incredible projects with you, too. These projects are not only fun but can be therapeutic.

Art is a spiritual practice that can help you connect your body to your inner being. It can help you create self-awareness and add meaning to your life. Think of the colors that represent your feelings today. What colors do your emotions radiate? If you can imagine an aura of colors around yourself, what colors would they be? If you're creating a project for a friend, what colors come to mind?

When you look at your raw canvas, disregard what it looks like now and remember it's about the bones. Never reject an item to upcycle due to its color, texture, or outdated look. If it's a piece of furniture, think of it as something about yourself that you want to fix. Put that energy into that inanimate object, healing all its flaws, taking its discarded form and transforming it into a valued, purposeful work of art.

When you start a project, do away with any preconceived notions and don't put restraints on yourself. You don't have to know exactly how you want it to turn out when you begin. I always say that I don't color the piece, the piece tells me how it wants to be colored. Let your subconscious be your guide. By tapping into your subconscious, you'll open up your spirituality and find a sense of direction that is a reflection of you. Art is within all of us, waiting to be released. Our special gift from God.

You'll find color suggestions for each project, but feel free to choose your own colors. Unicorn SPiT is not the same in my hand as it is in yours; it works like a magic scepter and releases the power you have within.

In this book, I'm going to help you find self-love through art. We will cover a range of mediums, from watercolor to refinishing furniture. You'll discover that there's always an easy way to fix an area you don't like, or to see it in a new light and embrace it. My goal is to help people activate the left and right side of their brain by creating balance and confidence even outside of the art studio or crafting space.

When I created Unicorn SPiT, I was skeptical of how it would be received. But after seeing the art created by thousands of people using the product, its powers have proved to be real. Follow along with me and let's create art pieces out of everyday objects that are also beautiful, touchable, shareable, and joyful reflections of ourselves. Welcome to an ARTiSTiC lifestyle you will love. Let those creative juices flow!

# CHAPTER ONE

# Getting Started with Unicorn SPiT

# Surface Preparation

Prep is always key! For best results, wood, glass, metal, fabric, concrete, pottery, wicker, and hard existing finishes must be prepared before applying Unicorn SPiT. When applying over existing painted, stained, and sealed surfaces, plastic, and glass, do the following.

1. Remove all dirt, grease, grime, waxy build-up, and oils with a cleaning agent.
2. Dishwasher-safe items can go in the dishwasher with detergent.
3. Lightly buff with grit sandpaper to degloss the surface. (This does not apply to glass.)
4. Wipe the surface with 71 percent or higher isopropyl to remove any residue or dust.
5. Allow it to dry.

## Staining Wood, Concrete, Clay, or Other Porous, Sealed Surfaces

1. Remove all dirt, grease, grime, waxy build-up, or oils with a cleaning or stripping agent.
2. Wipe the surface with 71 percent or higher isopropyl alcohol to remove any residue.
3. Sand or strip, exposing the raw substrate.
4. Remove sanding dust.

## Raw Wood, Raw Concrete, Raw Clay, Canvas, Paper, Fabric

1. Remove all stickers, labels, adhesives, and protective films. Make sure the fabrics are clean
2. Remove any dust.

## Determining Dilution Rates

To choose the dilution rate that fits your needs, prepare samples and test them on the same substrate as your project.

**How to Prepare Samples:**

1. Add 1 part Unicorn SPiT to a resealable container.
2. Add 1 part diluting agent to the container and mix well.
3. Apply a small amount of the mixture to the test surface.
4. Let it dry.
5. Seal.
6. Record the ratio and the result.
7. Repeat steps 2–6 on a clean test area, adding more diluting agent each time to find the dilution rate that suits your needs.

# Dilution Ratio Guide—Regular Unicorn SPiT

| Treatment/Application Type | Water/Water-Based Medium/Alcohol/ Epoxy Dilution Ratio |
|---|---|
| Paint/Heavy Glaze or Antiquing/Dry Brushing | 0–1 Part |
| Light Glaze/Light Whitewash/Light Antiquing | 0–3 Parts |
| Wood Stain (Bare Wood)/Dye for Stained Surfaces | 3–40 Parts |
| Fabric | 1–20 Parts |
| Concrete | 0–9 Parts |
| Glass | 0–15 Parts |
| Alcohol Ink | 10–40 Parts |
| Epoxy/Resin | 10–40 Parts |
| Pouring Medium | 4–10 Parts |

NOTE: SPARKLiNG is best used at full strength or diluted with up to 10 parts diluting agents.

## Recommended Diluting Agents

Mix these mediums with Unicorn SPiT to DiY other art mediums.

- Water
- Decoupage
- Water-based topcoat (interior and exterior)
- Fabric medium/E6000 Plus spray adhesive
- E6000 Fabri-Fuse
- 71 percent isopropyl alcohol
- Clear acrylic paint
- Epoxy/resin, like FAMOWOOD Glaze Coat
- Food-safe, water-based sealants
- Water-based concrete sealants
- Pouring medium

# Liquid-Wood Canvas/ Primer Concoction Formula

How to use FAMOWOOD Water-based White wood filler:

1. Mix wood-filler with filtered water until you get a cake batter-like consistency.
2. Apply that to your prepped surface using brushstrokes that complement the flow of your anticipated artwork.
3. Allow it to dry.

**NOTE:** You can buy premixed liquid wood canvas, but I've found that it clumps and dries out in the can and is expensive. So, I prefer to make my own using the formula above. Not only am I able to fix cracks, dents, and damage and create raised stencils, but it also has a hidden purpose: diluting its paste-like form to a brushable consistency allows the items to be stained instead of painted. This gives the surface a multidimensional effect that is similar to bare wood.

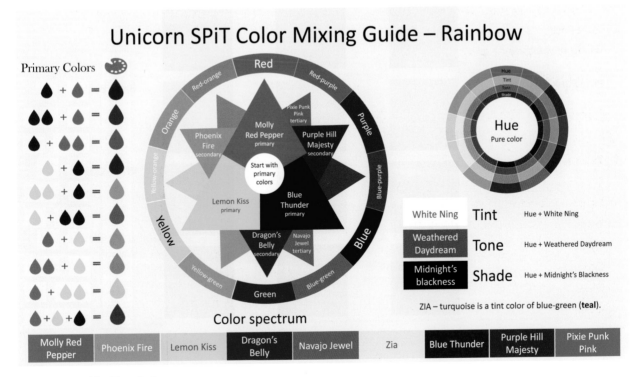

Chart created by Tamsin Lees.

# Unicorn SPiT on Different Types of Wood

When staining raw white softwoods like birch, white oak, balsa, pine, and more, the stain will be bright and remain true to color when wet, once sealed.

When staining raw hardwoods like oak, mahogany, walnut, or other dark/rich-colored woods, the stain will inherit the earth tones and turn out rich.

Dark-toned woods are hard, which means they won't absorb pigment as well as light-toned softwoods. I suggest diluting less when working with dark-toned woods. This leaves a thicker pigmentation on the surface as well as in the fine pores.

Here are some examples of SPiT on different types of wood after being sealed.

| Unicorn SPiT Color | Full Strength | Diluted with 3 Parts water | DIluted with 10 parts water | Wood Species |
|---|---|---|---|---|
| Molly Red Pepper | | | | Baltic Birch |
| | | | | White Oak |
| | | | | Walnut |
| Pixie Punk Pink | | | | Baltic Birch |
| | | | | White Oak |
| | | | | Walnut |

| Unicorn SPiT Color | Full Strength | Diluted with 3 Parts water | Diluted with 10 parts water | Wood Species |
|---|---|---|---|---|
| Phoenix Fire | | | | Baltic Birch |
| | | | | White Oak |
| | | | | Walnut |
| Lemon Kiss | | | | Baltic Birch |
| | | | | White Oak |
| | | | | Walnut |
| Zia | | | | Baltic Birch |
| | | | | White Oak |
| | | | | Walnut |

| Unicorn SPiT Color | Full Strength | Diluted with 3 Parts water | Diluted with 10 parts water | Wood Species |
|---|---|---|---|---|
| Navajo Jewel | | | | Baltic Birch |
| | | | | White Oak |
| | | | | Walnut |
| Dragon's Belly | | | | Baltic Birch |
| | | | | White Oak |
| | | | | Walnut |
| Blue Thunder | | | | Baltic Birch |
| | | | | White Oak |
| | | | | Walnut |

| Unicorn SPiT Color | Full Strength | Diluted with 3 Parts water | Diluted with 10 parts water | Wood Species |
|---|---|---|---|---|
| Purple Hill Majesty | | | | Baltic Birch |
| | | | | White Oak |
| | | | | Walnut |
| Midnight's Blackness | | | | Baltic Birch |
| | | | | White Oak |
| | | | | Walnut |
| Weathered Daydream | | | | Baltic Birch |
| | | | | White Oak |
| | | | | Walnut |

| Unicorn SPiT Color | Full Strength | Diluted with 3 Parts water | Diluted with 10 parts water | Wood Species |
|---|---|---|---|---|
| White Ning | | | | Baltic Birch |
| | | | | White Oak |
| | | | | Walnut |
| Rustic Reality | | | | Baltic Birch |
| | | | | White Oak |
| | | | | Walnut |
| SQUiRRELL | | | | Baltic Birch |
| | | | | White Oak |
| | | | | Walnut |

| SPARKLiNG Colors | One Coat | Two Coats | Wood Species |
|---|---|---|---|
| Dolly Firebird | | | Baltic Birch |
| | | | White Oak |
| | | | Walnut |
| Sapphire Swift | | | Baltic Birch |
| | | | White Oak |
| | | | Walnut |
| Violet Vulture | | | Baltic Birch |
| | | | White Oak |
| | | | Walnut |

| SPARKLiNG Colors | One Coat | Two Coats | Wood Species |
|---|---|---|---|
| Lavish Lovebirds | | | Baltic Birch |
| | | | White Oak |
| | | | Walnut |
| Starling Sasha | | | Baltic Birch |
| | | | White Oak |
| | | | Walnut |
| Golden Gosling | | | Baltic Birch |
| | | | White Oak |
| | | | Walnut |

# Unicorn SPiT to Oil Paint Matches

The mixtures below, created by Haley Sellmeyer, show full strength on the left and diluted with water on the right. Water was used as an alternative to paint thinner.

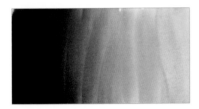

### Mountain Mixture

1 part Midnight's Blackness

1 part Molly Red Pepper

2 parts Blue Thunder

½ part Lemon Kiss

### Shadow Mixture

1 part Blue Thunder

½ part of Midnight's Blackness

1 part White Ning

### Parisian Blue

1 part Midnight's Blackness

3 parts Blue Thunder

½ part White Ning

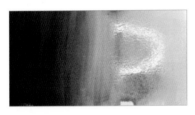

### Van Dyke Brown

1 part Midnight's Blackness

2 parts Phoenix

1 part Molly Red Pepper

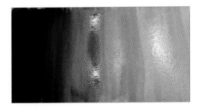

### Dark Sienna Brown

1 part Molly Red Pepper

1 part Phoenix

½ part Midnight's Blackness

1 part Lemon Kiss

### Cad Yellow

1 part Lemon Kiss

2 parts White Ning

### Brick Red

4 parts Molly Red Pepper

¼ part Midnight's Blackness

### Alizarin Crimson

4 parts Molly Red Pepper

⅛ part Midnight's Black

### Indian Yellow

3 parts Lemon Kiss

½ part Phoenix Fire

2 drops of Midnight's Blackness

### Bright Red

1 part Molly Red Pepper

1 part Phoenix Fire

### Yellow Ochre

1 part Lemon Kiss

½ part Phoenix Fire

⅛ part Midnight's Blackness

### Sap Green

1 part Midnight's Blackness

1 part Lemon Kiss

### Phthalo Green

2 parts Blue Thunder

1 part Dragon's Belly

### Phthalo Blue

5 parts Blue Thunder

1 part Dragon's Belly

# DiY Alcohol iNK Chart

| | 1:5 | 1:10 | 1:20 | 1:30 | 1:40 |
|---|---|---|---|---|---|
| Phoenix Fire Orange | | | | | |
| Pixie Punk Pink Magenta | | | | | |
| Molly Red Pepper Red | | | | | |
| Purple Hill Majesty Purple | | | | | |
| Blue Thunder Blue | | | | | |
| Weathered Daydream Gray | | | | | |
| Navajo Jewel Teal | | | | | |
| Zia Turquoise | | | | | |
| SQUiRREL Light Brown | | | | | |
| Dragon's Belly Green | | | | | |
| Rustic Reality Dark Brown | | | | | |
| Lemon Kiss Yellow | | | | | |
| Midnight's Blackness Black | | | | | |
| White Ning White | | | | | |

# Sealing

While sealing is not mandatory for all decorative projects, I advise it for durability and moisture protection. Follow the sealer manufacturer's directions and safety guidelines.

## Compatible Oil-based Sealers

- Interior oil-based sealants—polyurethane lacquer
- Finishing wax
- Sealing salves
- Beeswax
- Aerosol clear coat and lacquer
- Epoxy and resin
- Clear nail polish/UV gel topcoat
- Oil-based food-safe sealants
- Butcher block oil
- Exterior oil-based sealants
- Marine varnish
- Hard finishing wax
- Wood-penetrating and treatment oils
- Oil-based concrete sealer
- Automotive topcoat
- Hair spray
- Silicone waterproofing spray for fabric
- Clear chalkboard paint
- Clear frosted glass aerosol spray

## Results from Finishes

- Satin and matte topcoats will result in a one-dimensional effect.
- Gloss coats will achieve a semi-three-dimensional effect.
- High-gloss epoxy/resin, such as FAMOWOOD Glaze Coat, will achieve a significant three-dimensional effect.

## General Uses

### Laminated MDF or Poster Board

1. Surface prep: Clean the surface with a degreasing agent, and then rinse, removing any residue. Sand the cleaned surface lightly with 220-grit sandpaper to remove any gloss. Clean off the sanding dust and let it dry. A base coat of paint is not required.
2. Use an array of techniques to apply Unicorn SPiT.
3. Seal. I recommend sealing with your choice of non-water-based/oil-based topcoat other than wax or salves.

### Laminate Countertop Surfaces

1. Prepare the surface
2. Sand lightly with 220 grit sandpaper to remove any gloss.
3. Apply Unicorn SPiT. (A base coat of paint or primer is optional if you want a blank slate.)
4. Allow the artwork to dry/cure.
5. Seal: I recommend sealing countertops with an epoxy/resin, such as FAMOWOOD Glaze Coat.

### Glass Stain or Glass Paint

1. Prepare the surface.
2. For a semi-solid/non-transparent color, apply Unicorn SPiT directly to the prepared glass. For translucent results, mix 1 part Unicorn SPiT with 4–10 parts water-based decoupage before applying to the glass. The lower the ratio of Unicorn SPiT, the more the translucent effect. (Note: Colors will dull slightly in this "wet" stage but will return when they're cured and sealed.)
3. Apply it directly to the prepared glass.
4. Allow it to cure following the decoupage manufacturer's directions or until a solid chalky finish appears.
5. Seal with the appropriate sealer. For exterior use, use an exterior sealant. For interior use, use an interior sealer. For food-based items, use the appropriate sealer. Penetrating oils, salves, and waxes are not recommended to seal glass. You're going to want to use a stronger instant barrier protection like a spray or brush-on sealant, or even epoxy/resin. (Note: When using decoupage as the diluting agent, mix in a resealable container and allow bubbles to dissipate before use.)

### Automotive/Metal Paint

1. Prepare the surface (see page 2).
2. Sand the prepared surface lightly with 220-grit or higher sandpaper to remove any gloss if Unicorn SPiT is repelling application.
3. A base coat of primer is optional.
4. Apply Unicorn SPiT.
5. Seal with the appropriate topcoat.

### DiY Chalk Paste for Screen and Traditional Stencils

1. Prepare the surface (see page 2).
2. Mix Unicorn SPiT with stencil powder in a resealable container, following the manufacturer's directions.
3. Once the Unicorn SPiT has transformed into a fluffy chalk paste substance, apply the following traditional stenciling techniques.
4. Remove the stencil before the chalk paste is dry.
5. Easily remove the wet or dried product design from chalkboard or well-sealed surfaces with a damp cloth at your leisure.
6. No need to rush cleaning stencils and screens. Unicorn Spit with chalk paste will rise away and not harm them.
7. Seal your project to make it permanent.

### Fabric Paint or Dye—Ways to Apply

Apply the following directly to clean fabric by dipping, stamping, screen printing, soaking, tie-dyeing, brushing, stenciling, splattering, or spraying your fabric. Achieve permanent and semi-permanent results on common fabrics and knits.

**Washing:** Fabric will retain much of the Unicorn SPiT color if it is treated before washing (see various methods below). For best results, after allowing the project to dry for 24 hours, wash the finished product in cold water by hand (with very little detergent), then rinse with cold water.

## Semi-Permanent Fabric Coloring

Colors will fade gradually through each wash. Color transferring MAY occur. About 90 percent of the time, if you don't seal it, the color will wash out.

Here's a picture of the washcloths I use for my art. You can see how colorful they are after multiple washes.

However, I tried to stencil a pair of stretchy pants and it washed right out. I'm sure it had to do with the fabric type. You can do your own washcloth experiments and share them with our online group (see Resources).

### Diluting with Water

1. Mix 1 part Unicorn SPiT with 0–30 parts water. The lower the ratio of Unicorn SPiT, the better the translucent effect.
2. Apply.
3. Heat set using the following color setting methods below. This will not change the texture, durability, or feel of the fabric.
   - **Hair dryer:** Let Unicorn SPiT dry. Using the hottest hair dryer setting to heat the fabric until the fabric is hot. Allow it to cool to room temperature.
   - **Iron:** Let Unicorn SPiT dry. Put your iron on the hottest setting (without moisture) that's recommended for the fabric type.

Lay parchment paper over the fabric. Iron the front and back of the fabric until it's hot. Allow it to cool to room temperature.

- **Clothes Dryer:** Place your dried project in the dryer on the hottest setting for one hour. Remove and allow it to cool to room temperature.

4. Let your project set for 24 hours before use or rinse.

### Permanent Fabric Coloring

Color transferring may NOT occur.

#### Fabric Medium/E6000 Spray Adhesive:

1. Mix 1 part Unicorn SPiT with 1–30 parts fabric medium or E6000 Spray Adhesive.
2. Apply.
3. Allow the colorant to cure before using. Follow the fabric manufacturer's directions before use or dry it with a hair dryer at the highest possible setting until dry (heat set). **Optional:** Apply a second coat of untreated (clear) fabric medium for high-traffic surfaces, like upholstered furniture. (Note: This may change the texture, durability, and feel of the fabric.)

#### E6000 Fabri-Fuse (DiY Fabric Paint/Ink for screen printing, stenciling, and stamping)

1. Mix 1 part Unicorn SPiT with 1–3 parts E6000 Fabri-Fuse.
2. Apply your desired design.
3. Dry flat naturally or dry it with a hair dryer at the highest possible setting until it's dry (heat set). It should be washable after 72 hours. Note: This will change the texture and feel of the fabric on the areas it is applied.

#### Fabric Protectant Spray/ Fabric Waterproofing Spray

1. Apply Unicorn SPiT (diluted or full-strength) directly to the fabric.
2. Allow to dry.
3. Apply interior or exterior silicone waterproofing spray protectant to your dried project.

4. Allow it to cure, following the manufacturer's directions before use. Apply a second coat of fabric protectant spray to high-traffic surfaces such as upholstered furniture, fashion accessories, and footwear. (Note: This will *not* drastically change the texture, durability, or feel of the fabric.)

# Medium Uses

Complete the surface preparation and then apply the following Unicorn SPiT applications to painted, sealed, or bare surfaces including—but not limited to—metal, pottery, concrete, ceramics, plastic, laminate, paper, fabric, and leather.

**Directions for use as a paint, glaze, or antiquing/ dry brushing on non-porous/sealed wood, glass, metal, fabric, pottery, wicker, concrete, and laminate.**

1. Use Unicorn SPiT right out of the bottle for a color application or dilute it with up to 3 parts water for antiquing or dry brushing. Diluting Unicorn SPiT allows you to control the opaqueness. For antiquing or dry brushing, add 1 part Unicorn SPiT in a resealable container and dilute with water. Test the dilution on a small, dry, clean sample piece of the same substrate as your project. Gradually add up to 3 parts of water until the desired effect is achieved.
2. Let it dry until a chalky finish appears. Drying time ranges from 3 minutes to 72 hours, depending on the material, humidity, and temperature.
3. Apply the diluted Unicorn SPiT to the surface after it is completely void of all oil, dirt, grime, or anything that may inhibit the product from making contact with the surface to antique, age, color, highlight, or lowlight.
4. Continue to add or blend multiple colors to the surface in separate areas, creating designs to achieve your desired look.
5. Optional: After drying, lightly buff the surface with a fine grain sandpaper (220 or higher grit), extra-fine steel wool, or a damp cloth

to remove to reveal more of the substrate, if desired.

6. Dust it off thoroughly.

7. Seal with any oil-based coating/sealer. For best protection, repeat coats of sealer as indicated on the product's instructions.

**DiY Self-Sealing Stain**

1. Use 3–40 parts water-based topcoat to 1 part Unicorn SPiT.

2. Brush onto bare wood with even thickness.

3. Allow it to absorb.

4. Wipe off the excess with a lint-free cloth.

5. Allow it to dry.

6. For added durability, seal it again using an untreated clear top coat that has no pigment, either water-based or oil-based. For best protection, repeat coats of sealer as indicated on the product's instructions.

**Directions for use as a self-sealing glaze, white or color wash, or antiquing agent.**

1. Dilute Unicorn SPiT with up to 5 parts of a clear water-based medium to make a light glaze, whitewash, or antiquing agent. Diluting Unicorn SPiT with water-based medium allows you to control the opaqueness. Add 1 part Unicorn SPiT in a resealable container to be diluted with water. Test the dilution on a small, dry, clean sample piece of the same substrate as your project, gradually adding up to 3 parts of water until you achieve the desired effect.

2. Apply the diluted Unicorn SPiT to the surface after it is completely void of all oil, dirt, grime, or anything that may inhibit the product from making contact with the surface to antique, age, color, highlight, or lowlight.

3. Continue to add or blend multiple colors to the surface in separate areas, creating designs to achieve your desired look.

4. Before dried, use a soft (dry or damp) cloth to polish away excess Unicorn SPiT until you've achieved your desired effect.

5. Allow it to dry following the water-based diluting agent recommendations.

6. For best protection, repeat coats of sealer as indicated on the product's instructions.

**Directions for use as a dry/hard watercolor.**

1. Refill watercolor palettes with Unicorn SPiT.

2. Allow the mixture to dry or freeze.

3. Apply your mixture with traditional dry/hard watercolor techniques.

(**NOTE:** Remember that Unicorn SPiT has a higher concentration of pigmentation than some of the most expensive watercolors on the market.)

**Directions for use as a gel or liquid watercolor.**

1. Use Unicorn SPiT in place of gel or liquid watercolor.

2. Apply Unicorn SPiT with traditional gel or liquid watercolor techniques but use more water as it is very potent.

3. Apply Unicorn SPiT colors using common liquid watercolor practices.

**Directions for use as a non-self-sealing wood stain or dye.**

1. Prepare the surface.

2. Mist the raw wood surface with water to open the pores. You don't need a wood conditioner if the wood is not at risk of cracking due to dryness.

3. Dilute Unicorn SPiT up to 40 parts water to make the stain. Diluting with water allows you to control the opaqueness and absorption into the porous surface. You can pre-dilute, or dilute as you go with a wet brush or a spray bottle of water.

4. Add 1 part Unicorn SPiT in a resealable container to be diluted with water. Test the dilution on a small, dry, clean sample piece of the same substrate as your project, gradually adding up to 40 parts water until the desired effect is achieved.

5. Let it dry until a chalky finish appears. Drying time is approximately 3 minutes to 48 hours, depending on the material, humidity, and temperature.

6. After drying, lightly buff the surface with fine-grit sandpaper (220+ grit) or extra-fine steel wool (following the grain) to give it a distressed or worn look if desired.

7. Dust thoroughly.

8. If the grain feels raised, lightly buff the surface with clean cardboard to smooth the texture.

9. Seal with any oil-based coating/sealer or epoxy, like FAMOWOOD Glaze Coat. For better protection, repeat coats of the sealer as indicated on the product instructions. High-gloss sealers will help you achieve a three-dimensional look.

### Directions for use as an alcohol ink.

1. Prepare the surface.

2. Mix Unicorn SPiT with 10–40 parts 71 percent isopropyl alcohol. (Note: A higher alcohol ratio will achieve a lighter pigment. A lower alcohol ratio will achieve a deeper/stronger pigment.)

3. Mix well.

4. Mix the colors to achieve custom colors.

5. Apply using common alcohol ink practices.

6. Seal using common alcohol ink practices.

### Directions for use as an epoxy/resin tint.

1. Prepare the surface.

2. Mix the epoxy or resin per the manufacturer's directions.

3. Add 1 part Unicorn SPiT to 10–40 parts epoxy/resin immediately at the start of your allotted working time. (The lower ratio of Unicorn SPiT results in a more translucent effect.)

4. Stir the mixture until it's fully incorporated.

5. Apply to your piece.

6. Allow your project to cure/harden, according to the epoxy/resin manufacturer's directions.

### Directions for use in flow/fluid art.

1. Mix 1 part Unicorn SPiT and ¼ parts water, with 4–10 parts paint extender/pouring medium. The lower the ratio of Unicorn SPiT, the more translucent the effect. (Colors will dull slightly in this "wet" stage but turn vibrant again once cured and sealed.)

2. Adding a few drops of cell activator or silicone lubricants to create large cells is optional. Unicorn SPiT creates small cells naturally due to the existing scented oil.

3. Apply the flow mixture to the prepared surface.

4. Allow your project to cure/harden until a solid chalky finish appears. It can take from 12 to 72 hours, depending on the material, humidity, and temperature.

5. There's no need to powder and clean oil off unless pooling of added cell activator or silicone lubricant is present.

6. Seal with any oil-based coating/sealer or epoxy, like FAMOWOOD Glaze Coat. For better protection, repeat coats of the sealer as indicated on the product instructions. High-gloss sealers will help you achieve a three-dimensional look.

## Why Is It Best to Use Unicorn SPiT in Pours and Flow Art?

1. Unicorn SPiT comes in a concentrate unlike any other pigmented medium on the market.

2. It's cost-friendly, especially when you use 4–10 parts pouring medium to 1 part Unicorn SPiT, as opposed to equal parts, as you would with plastic-based paints such as acrylic or latex.

3. Unicorn SPiT already contains aromatherapy oil; it's emulsified within its structure, which is why the oil doesn't float on top. So, when doing a pour, you will automatically get cells creating visual interest. Plus, it makes your whole room smell amazing!

4. It has a controllable cell size. If you want very large cells, add extra silicone oil or cell activator. Hitting the pour with a flame, before it sets up, makes more cells than without the flame.

5. You avoid the extra steps you have to take with acrylic, latex, and plastic-based paints that you need to add silicone to get cells. They also need to be dusted down with powders to absorb the residual cell activator or agents.

Plastic-based paints turn into plastic upon drying, blocking silicone from absorbing. The residual cell activator or silicone residue will also repel topcoats, even epoxy, if not removed.

6. Unicorn SPiT requires fewer steps because it doesn't contain any plastics. Small amounts of added silicone or cell activator will absorb into SPiT. This makes epoxying and topcoating a breeze.

7. The dry time is quick! Unicorn SPiT pours can be topcoated or epoxied in as few as 12 hours, unlike plastic-based paints that require as long as 90 days. The difference is Unicorn SPiT has no plastics to trap moisture. It dries easily, becoming moisture-free. This eliminates the risk of bubbles, fog, mildew, mold, lifting, and peeling down the road.

8. You get this amazing 3D-effect that you simply can't get with any other medium on the market.

9. Unicorn SPiT takes you to a magical place where you know your artwork is safe.

# Basic Techniques

Try these basic techniques on any prepared surface.

### Dry Brushing

1. Prepare the surface.
2. Apply straight or diluted Unicorn SPiT with a dry or damp, frayed brush, grazing the surface and leaving most or some of the original finish exposed.
3. Seal with appropriate topcoat, depending on use.

### Antiquing

1. Prepare the surface.
2. Apply Unicorn SPiT straight or diluted to a sealed surface.
3. Allow it to dry until a chalky finish appears. The dry time is approximately 3 minutes to 48 hours, depending on the material, humidity, and temperature.
4. Once dry, remove the excess Unicorn SPiT from the previously sealed detail areas with a dry or damp cloth, if desired.
5. Seal with appropriate topcoat, depending on use.

### Color Washing and Glazing

1. Prepare the surface.
2. Apply single or multiple diluted and non-diluted Unicorn SPiT colors to the painted or sealed surface with flattering brush strokes.
3. Allow it to dry until a chalky finish appears. The dry time is approximately 3 minutes to 48 hours, depending on the material, humidity, and temperature.
4. Seal with appropriate topcoat, depending on use.

### Stain Press

1. Prepare the surface.
2. Mist the surface with water.
3. Apply Unicorn SPiT directly to the surface in a random or organized and spaced pattern.
4. Mist with water.
5. Cover the surface with clear plastic wrap.
6. Mist the plastic wrap with water.
7. Manipulate the Unicorn SPiT under the plastic wrap with your hands or a roller to cover the surface.
8. Peel off the plastic wrap in a direction that matches the flow of your design. This articulates a flow in the pigment that's left behind and enhances the appearance of movement in your design.
9. Mist the surface with water to blend or apply more Unicorn SPiT and stain-press it again if desired.
10. Allow it to dry.
11. Seal with appropriate topcoat, depending on use.

### Laminated Countertops, MDF, or Poster Board

1. Buff the prepared surface lightly with 220-grit or higher sandpaper to remove any gloss.
2. Apply Unicorn SPiT. A base coat of paint or primer is optional.
3. Seal. I recommend sealing countertops with an epoxy/resin, such as FAMOWOOD Glaze Coat. For surfaces other than countertops, feel free to seal them with your choice of high traffic, non-water-based topcoats.

# Unicorn SPiT Tips to Remember

- Create mixed media art by intermingling paint finishes, plaster, decoupage, textures, mediums, stamps, inks, metallic mediums, markers, or spray paint in combination with Unicorn SPiT to achieve unique finishes.
- Most water-based paints (chalk, mineral, acrylic, or latex-based) can be tinted with Unicorn SPiT to create custom colors.
- Mix various colors of Unicorn SPiT to create custom colors.
- Unicorn SPiT (when not mixed with a water-based coating) can dry in your brushes, stencils, tools, and palettes without damaging them. Water easily washes Unicorn SPiT away, or wet your brush, cloth, or pallet to utilize the remaining pigment. There's no need to rush and clean.
- When cleaning, Unicorn SPiT can safely be washed away easily and without fear of harming the environment.
- Topcoats must be oil-based when you're not mixing with a water-based medium. Using a water-based topcoat on untreated Unicorn SPiT will alter the look and may lift or smear.
- To create various varnishes, intermingle chalky paint finishes, acrylic paint, plaster, decoupage, metallic mediums, or metallic spray paint with Unicorn SPiT.
- Whether you work in an art studio or at your kitchen table, set the ambiance. Put on inspiring music, light your favorite scented candle, and make sure you keep your drink cup separate from your brush cup. I can't tell you how many times I've picked up my brush cup thinking it was my drink cup.

# CHAPTER TWO

# Wood Dye and Stain

Trees shade us and give us oxygen. We climb them and swing on them to play. They create a beautiful ambiance wherever they grow. They also die for us. Let's relish how trees warm us, create walls for us to live in, and furniture for us to rest upon. I learned my deep appreciation of wood from the folks at the day-care center. To me, the value of wood is greater than any human-made product.

I was taught that wood without damage should never be painted. Many people desire to have color, and with Unicorn SPiT, you don't have to sacrifice the beautiful wood grain to satisfy your thirst for color. You can make anything look like rainbow eucalyptus or make it one solid color if you want, without compromising the natural beauty of the wood, which should be shown off in thanks for all that it does.

Here, I will show you the different ways to showcase every single ring of that tree and pay it the homage it deserves. In the following projects, we will be adding color to a bare wood surface.

# Americana Wood Blocks

With this project, I'm going to show you how to trace the lines of the wood grain in colors that represent what you would like to convey. You don't need to be perfect, precise, or even neat. You don't have to worry about putting it on too thick or too thin, for the brushing at the end will allow all of your colors to blend. I call this the Mariposa technique.

# Directions

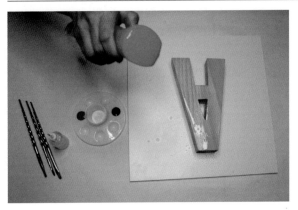

1. To prepare the wood, use 220-grit sandpaper and sand any rough edges. Then dust off the pieces.

2. Mist the wood pieces with clean water, which works in place of a conditioner. This opens the pores and gets the wood ready to absorb the pigment. Just damp, not dripping.

3. Wet your brush with water. Have a little cup of clean water nearby. Dilute the Unicorn SPiT to the strength that you desire, testing on a piece of paper if you like. For this, I used about 5 parts water to 1 part SPiT for the Molly Red Pepper and Blue Thunder.

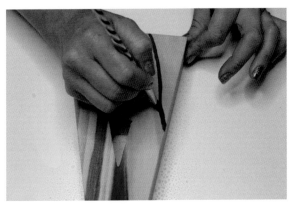

4. Begin with your first color, following the grain pattern. Count every third line and apply a stripe of color.

5. After you've applied Blue Thunder, you're going to want to follow alongside it with the Molly Red Pepper. Make sure you continue the ring if it goes along the back and sides.

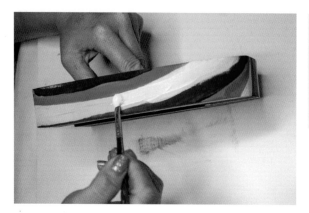

### PRO TIP

- When using white, I like to use it full strength and not diluted, to get a rich color. I think this is the only color of Unicorn SPiT I hardly ever dilute.

**6.** Fill the gaps in between with White Ning at full strength.

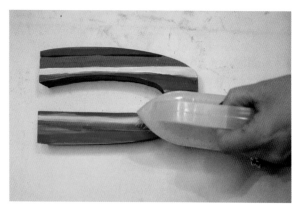

**7.** Once dry, use a stiff, dry scrub brush to buff the colors following the direction of the grain lines until the colors fade together. This is as opposed to having a drastic sharp line if you want it more blended.

**8.** Once dusted off, you can go through and add some highlight pinstriping here and there like I did, using the concept color Zeus.

**9.** Feel free to seal with any oil-based sealer appropriate for either indoor or outdoor use. Or you can make it dry dust only like I did, and you don't have to seal it.

# Boho Woodburning Tissue Box

Teachers, doctors, lawyers, and parents alike can appreciate the nurturing value in a simple tissue box. This solid wood tissue box from Walnut Hollow can be embellished in a way to suit your personality. We will be using SPARKLiNG Unicorn SPiT as well as traditional Unicorn SPiT and outlining the images with woodburning techniques. This will really take the tissue box from mundane to extraordinary.

## Items you will need:

- Array of Unicorn SPiT colors
- Bare wood tissue box (Walnut Hollow)
- Woodburning set (Walnut Hollow)
- Lead pencil
- Spray bottle of water
- Fine artist brushes
- Oil-based topcoat

# Directions

1. Measure the sides of the box and make a paper template for your design. Then sketch your design on the paper. Use carbon paper or homemade carbon paper (shade the whole sheet of paper with a pencil). You could also freehand your design if you desire.

2. Trace your design on the box revealing a light outline you can fill it in like a coloring book.

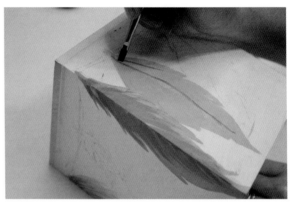

3. Select your colors of Unicorn SPiT. Apply a pea-sized drop to your palette and mist it with water to dilute it as you go.

4. Color in the design with the lightest color first, creating a color pattern of your choice.

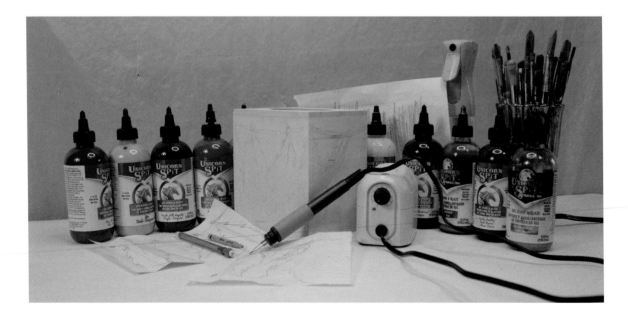

**5.** Add some dimension to your design by applying a coordinating darker tone over the lighter color base. For these, I used wispy, long, and strong strokes to make the feathers look airy.

**6.** Use your liner brush to create wide bands of detail like I did on the string that holds all the feathers together.

**7.** To create dimension, use SPARKLiNG Unicorn SPiT as the background to fill in any missing spaces.

**8.** Time to burn. Embellish your design by outlining the feathers with your wood burner. You can also use other woodburning tips to create shapes and shading.

**9.** Seal with your preferred oil-based topcoat.

## PRO TIPS

- Creating dimension by using regular Unicorn SPiT as the feature and SPARKLiNG SPiT as the background (or vice versa) gives amazing dimension very easily.
- You can burn before or after you apply color because Unicorn SPiT is free of plastics.

# Wood Flowers

## Items you'll need:

- Arrays of regular and SPARKLiNG Unicorn SPiT colors
- Concept color Zeus
- Uncolored sola wood flowers
- Vessel big enough in which to dip the flowers
- Spray bottle of water to dilute
- Small, 2 oz. spray bottle to mist color
- Skewers

Solid wood flowers are created by gathering precisely cut wood shavings. Many people use sola wood flowers for embellishing cards, wedding cake toppers, hair barrettes, boutonnieres, and bouquets. There isn't a place where a wooden flower wouldn't look adorable. In this project, I will show you some basic steps for how to create flowers that can last forever. There are some extraordinary artists that use Unicorn SPiT to create elaborate wood flowers professionally. I encourage you to be inspired by their works, which you can find on our online forum. I'm going to give you the basics. I won't be surprised if you can instantly surpass my abilities on these little wooden jewels.

# Directions

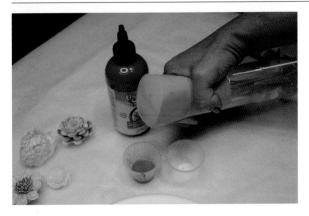

1. Create the wood dye using regular and SPARKLiNG Unicorn SPiT. For regular, mix 1 part Unicorn SPiT to 10–15 parts water, depending on how dark you want the tone to be. For SPARKLiNG, dilute 1-part SPARKLiNG Unicorn SPiT to 5 parts water, depending on how deep you want the color tone.

2. Push a skewer into the bottom of the flower to serve as a handle. The petals are delicate, so try to keep your fingers off them as much as possible.

3. Dip the flower into the Unicorn SPiT water mixture until fully submerged.

4. Remove flowers after a few seconds allowing excess to drip back into your dye cup.

## PRO TIP

- Feel free to get crafty and drip different colors on a flower to create a tie-dyed look, or use a fine brush or airbrush to articulate your flowers with colorful detail. You can also mist them with aromatherapy oil to use as a diffuser.

**5.** Embellish with a small mister filled with gilding spray that is 1 part concept color Zeus to 10 parts water.

**6.** Remove the flower from the skewer and allow your flowers to dry face-side up.

**7.** There's no need to seal as the color absorbs and will not rub off. Sola wood flowers are meant to be treated the same as any dried flower but are more durable.

# Mahogany-Colored Shot Box

Keepsake boxes are a great way to package a gift or become a gift on its own. In this project, I will teach you how to make a self-sealing stain in a custom color, and then how to embellish it with embossing powder. Whether you give this as a gift to a groomsman or your bourbon-loving friends, this customized gift is a spin on a traditional keepsake. It will put a smile on their face and be a constant reminder of the good times.

## What you'll need:

- Unicorn SPiT colors: Molly Red Pepper, Rustic Reality, Midnight's Blackness
- Syringe for measurement
- Wide, flat brush
- Blush brush
- E6000 glue
- Screen stencil of your choice
- Resealable container
- Shop cloth
- Clear, water-based sealer
- Embossing tool
- Embossing powder
- Dishwasher-safe decoupage
- One shell casing
- Five projectiles or six shell casings

# Directions

1. Add 30 parts clear water-based topcoat, 4 parts Molly Red Pepper, 8 parts Rustic Reality, and 2 parts Midnight's Blackness.

2. Stir using your wide, flat brush. Mix thoroughly. This will create a self-sealing stain.

3. Apply the self-sealing stain using brush strokes following the flow of the grain pattern.

4. Dip your washcloth into the clear sealer.

5. Wipe the wet, freshly applied pigment with the water-based sealer and blend the colorant, wiping off excess. Remember to follow the grain. This will provide a second coat of sealer and reveal a beautiful mahogany color.

**6.** When the box is dry, place your screen stencil where desired, making sure there are no bubbles or wrinkles on the stencil that would compromise full contact with the wood. Apply a few drops of dishwasher-safe decoupage onto the stencil. Use a plastic card to scrape the decoupage across the stencil, allowing the decoupage to create the design on the surface.

**7.** Remove the stencil while the decoupage is wet.

**8.** Pour metallic embossing powder onto the wet stenciled design and allow it to dry 10–20 minutes, depending on humidity.

**9.** Dump the embossing powder off and lightly brush off any excess using a soft, poofy brush. I prefer blush brushes for this.

**10.** Once the excess embossing powder has been removed, use your embossing heat tool to melt the remaining powder, revealing a foil-like design.

**11.** Use E6000 Plus to attach the shell casing to the center of the design, which will act as your door hardware. Allow that casing to cure.

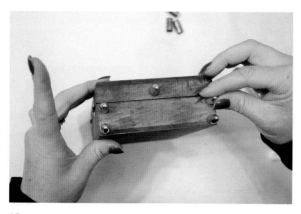

**12.** Use E6000 Plus to adhere the projectiles to the bottom to create feet for the box.

**13.** When the glue is dry, the shot box is ready to be filled with your favorite miniature liquor bottles.

## PRO TIP

- You can make wipe-on self-sealing wood stains in any color you like and in a hue as deep as you want, depending on the amount of clear coat you use. You can mix with an indoor and outdoor water-based sealant. You can also use tint-colored, self-sealing stains you may already own, with just a few splashes of Unicorn SPiT, to create a custom color. The color mixing guide on page 3 will give you all the color-mixing recipes your heart may desire.

# Beach Shading

Life's a beach! We all love the cool sand between our toes, the water washing onto the shore, and the way the blues blend into richer tones the deeper the water gets. In this project, I will show you how to obtain different depths and tones of blue with just one color. By gradually diluting the color, it will magically fade into the natural wood tone that will represent the sands. This may take you back to some of the best days of your life, which we all agree could be on a beach.

## What you'll need:

- Unicorn SPiT colors: White Ning and Blue Thunder
- Small piece of white pine wood router engraved with your favorite saying
- 220 grit sanding block
- Shop cloth
- Spray bottle of water

# Directions

1. Color in the grooves using White Ning in full strength. Apply liberally, as you want the white to be vibrant. Allow it to dry.

2. Once it's dry, use the sanding block to remove any stain that may have gone outside of the lines. Be sure to sand with the grain and not against it. Then dust it off.

3. Wrap the cloth around your finger for pinpoint accuracy, then mist your cloth with water. Dip your clothed finger into the Blue Thunder and gradually buff the stain into the grain. The most concentrated area will be in the bottom right-hand corner.

4. Working your way to the upper left-hand corner, you will see the pigment gradually start to run out, creating a lighter tone of blue as you blend it into the natural tone of the wood.

## PRO TIP

- Starting with less color and building it up by adding more color is easier to do than starting with too much color and having to sand it off. You will also be amazed at how many different tones of blue you will achieve, because Unicorn SPiT plays with the natural tone in the wood, creating a multifaceted effect.

**5.** If you find that you have a stark transition of color from the blue to the natural tone, wrap a clean part of the cloth around your finger and mist it with water.

**6.** Use the clean, wet part of the cloth to blend the stark line, making the tone lighter as you go. But be sure to leave an almost equal amount of the natural tone of the wood to represent sand beaches.

**7.** Allow it to dry.

**8.** You can seal with the appropriate sealer depending on where you're going to display it. Or you can make it dry-dust only.

# Kick up your design with tinted epoxy!

## What you'll need and how to prepare your setup:

- Unicorn SPiT Navajo Jewel, Blue Thunder, Zia, and White Ning
- FAMOWOOD Glaze Coat (resin/epoxy)
- Four disposable plastic cups
- Two wood picture frames
- Embossing heat tool
- Plastic drop cloth
- Risers

# Directions

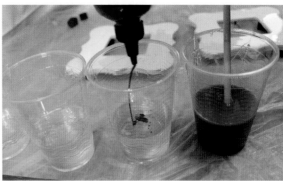

1. Prepare and protect your table by covering it with a plastic drop cloth. Make sure it's level. Put risers underneath the sign and frames.

2. Mix your resin/epoxy according to the directions on the bottle.

3. Pour the mixed epoxy into four separate cups, filling them about halfway. Then tint each cup a different color with Unicorn SPiT. The formula I used is 1 part Unicorn SPiT to 12 parts epoxy. Stir until the color is fully incorporated into the epoxy. Reserve one-fifth of the clear epoxy for making waves.

4. To create waves, pour clear epoxy on the entire sign. Allow it to flow over the edges.

5. Sparingly pour the White Ning-tinted epoxy in stripes where the Blue Thunder and the natural wood tone meet.

6. Create a couple of thin stripes moving downward toward the darkest blue. Allow to settle.

7. Use the embossing heat tool to move the white epoxy from side to side, creating the look of sea surf.

# Making coordinating picture frames

## Directions

**1.** Pour alternating stripes of epoxy tinted with Blue Thunder, Navajo Jewel, and Zia onto the frames.

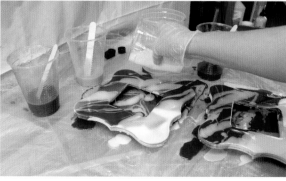

**2.** Drizzle your desired amount of the remaining White Ning tinted epoxy in thin bands across the thick colored stripes, following the same direction.

**3.** Pick up your frames and tilt them side to side to make the colors flow over the edges to cover the entire frame and sides. Place the frames on the risers and allow the epoxied items to cure and harden for as many hours as the manufacturer recommends.

**4.** The next day, use a heat gun and a metal putty knife to remove excess drips from the back.

### PRO TIP

· Take a large picture frame and cover with a plastic drop cloth to create a dam so no epoxy can escape your workspace.

# Mermaid Jewelry Box

As the saying goes, one person's trash is another person's treasure. When you go to thrift stores, there is an abundance of solid wood jewelry armoires to choose from. Most of them are 1970s and '80s brown, but they're generally solid wood and easy to prep. You can use a stripper to remove the existing finish. Sandpaper or even a soda blaster can reveal some expensive, exotic woods for pennies.

In this project, I will show you how to take this elaborate elm wood jewelry armoire and give it a fantasy spin that's bright, vibrant, and sparkles like a mermaid.

## What you'll need.

- SPARKLiNG Unicorn SPiT colors: Violet Vulture, Sapphire Swift, and Lavish Lovebirds
- Concept color: Zeus
- Stripping agent
- Artist brushes
- High-gloss topcoat
- Shop cloth
- Painter's tape
- Small, size-appropriate screwdriver

# Directions

1. Remove all metal hardware (drawer pulls and hinges if you can—I was unable to remove the hinges).

2. Apply the stripping agent liberally to all the areas you want to remove any sealer.

3. You can wrap the stripping agent-covered surfaces with plastic to keep them from drying out so it can do its work. Follow the stripping agent's brand directions. Make sure that you remove the stripping agent thoroughly from the surface and let it dry.

4. Place drawers back into the box and close the door so that it is set up as it would be when it's completed. Now, it's ready to stain.

**5.** Starting with Violet Vulture, apply the stain undiluted on one of the bottom corners with your brush. Concentrate on blending the color out toward the edges.

**6.** Once you've applied the deepest shade, use a wet brush to the darker edges to create an ombre effect from the dark purple to the natural wood. This will stretch out the color like we did earlier in the beach sign project (page 35).

**7.** Have the purple gradually shift into Sapphire Swift by starting the blue on a fresh area where the purple has not been. Then use a water-wet brush to activate the blue pigment and fade it into the purple. Use a clean, wet brush to activate the blue and fade it into the natural wood tone.

**8.** Mix a custom color of SPARKLiNG by following the color chart (page 3) to make teal.

**9.** Follow the same process as in step 7 to apply the custom teal. Continue alternating colors until you've achieved the ombre effect along the whole surface.

**10.** For the top, I chose to do half in Violet Vulture and half in the teal, blending the colors where they meet. I used a clean wet brush to activate both pigments until they seamlessly faded into each other. Allow your piece to dry.

**11.** Seal with your preferred oil-based high gloss topcoat. Allow it to cure following the manufacturer's directions.

**12.** Now, you're going to add shimmer and sparkle by filling the grain with gold. Using a brush, apply Zeus to an entire surface.

**13.** Using a soft, dry cloth, buff the Zeus while it's still wet. Small wiping strokes following the grain pattern will push the metallic micas into the pores of the grain.

**14.** Load a small, stiff brush with Zeus. Dry-brush the metallic gold color onto the raised architectural detail by lightly casting the tips of the brush to the highest peaks of the surface. Feel free to use a dampened Q-tip or cloth to remove any excess.

**15.** Once the gold grain filling and gold dry brushing of the architectural details are to your satisfaction, seal again as before.

**16.** After the topcoat is dry, replace all of the hardware.

## PRO TIPS

- When picking out jewelry boxes, don't let clear plastic-faced doors deter you. You can leave the glass or plastic as is, but remember, you can spruce up the glass or plexiglass to make it look like stained glass as well.

- Don't be shy with the gold highlighting. Remember you can always wipe it off and reapply it because it's not permanent until it's sealed. So, it's important to do the gold highlighting and accenting after the first topcoat has been applied and cured. This makes it easy to correct any mistakes.

# Abstract Wood Stain Fine Art

## What you'll need

- Unicorn SPiT colors: Lemon Kiss, Phoenix Fire, Zeal Teal, White Ning, Pixie Punk Pink, Purple Hill Majesty, Molly Red Pepper, Blue Thunder, Dragon's Belly, Navajo Jewel, and Midnight's Blackness
- Concept color: Hades
- Pair of well-fitting protective gloves
- Eye protection
- 320-grit sandpaper
- Sanding block
- ½" or thicker, light-colored wood or plywood with a pretty grain pattern
- Spray bottle of water
- Lint-free paper towels or shop cloths
- Palette or dish for water

Simulacrum is when you can find familiar shapes and everyday objects in nature like faces and animals. I tend to look at the grains in sheets of plywood in this way; I have always envisioned that it looks like either the sea or the sky. It's like God grew a perfect coloring book for us.

Susi Schuele is here to show you how she colors in the grain in a more abstract way that seems to just spring from her being.

# Directions

1. The first step in my process is to select the wood for my art. The grain is of particular importance to me. In this piece, there were some interesting natural darker grain areas that I felt would fit right into my design. I also used the "wrong" side of this wood because I liked the grain design better. I'll talk about each of the tools assembled here as I used them.

2. Sand the wood with 200- to 400-grit sandpaper. I am also using the wrong side of this board so there are very fine wood fibers that stick up. I always try to sand those out so I don't end up with them embedded in my fingers.

3. After you sand the board, use a sturdy rag and wipe it down to remove any sawdust residue.

4. Use two small drops of Lemon Kiss. You won't believe how far this will go. I always start with small amounts and add more as I need it or spray with water to extend it.

**5.** Next, add Phoenix Fire. Add a larger line for a brighter, bigger area and put it on top of the blended Lemon Kiss. My plan for this piece was to try and use as many of the Unicorn SPiT's primary and legendary colors as possible.

**6.** Add the third light color, Zia, to the top. Zia has an opaque tendency. I use this color almost as sparingly as I do the White Ning. But I thought it would be cool at the top of this piece.

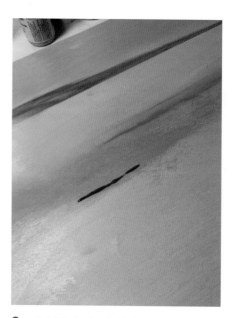

**7.** Blending is going on. Notice the dark grain between the Zia and the Lemon Kiss. It's creating its own design naturally. Also note the slight green tint formed by blending a bit of the Zia into the Lemon Kiss.

**8.** Add Pixie Punk Pink.

**9.** The Pixie Punk is blended into the Phoenix Fire above it. I didn't use much pink—it's really vibrant on bare wood but will dull when it is blended with another color. I have kept the dark grain so far and added a little bit of Lemon Kiss under it. You can see the water on the board as I really start to spray and blend.

**10.** Purple Hill Majesty was a great choice over the dark grain, as it added to the depth. I put this on pretty thick and haven't started to do the major blending that I normally do. That usually comes at the end of the piece after most of the color has been placed.

**11.** I do a lot of the "pulling" throughout my many artworks, and they have become signatures for my work.

## PRO TIPS

- One of my most critical tools is my spray bottle of water. I use the bottled water because I want it to be free of any possible tap sediment or minerals.

- To avoid spraying water into areas I don't want it to go, especially if they are small areas that need the water, I set aside a small dish of water and dip my gloved fingers into it to get them wet enough to reactivate and move the stain in very specific areas.

- I wet each segment before I apply the SPiT. Sometimes, depending on how vibrant I want the color, I might not use water. Other times, when I really want to dilute or fade the color, I add more water. In this piece, I was adding water generally before every application of SPiT. Sometimes I put the SPiT down first and sprayed it. Water is critical for my blending process.

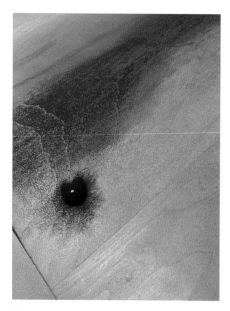

**12.** Put down a good-size drop of Molly Red Pepper. This is what it looks like when you put the stain down first and then add water to it. You can see the stain start to spread out.

**13.** Add Blue Thunder, another dark color, to the other side for some contrast. Note the grain in this picture. This is one of the most beautiful things about doing art on wood—enhancing the grain with Unicor SPiT's beautiful colors. The grain will remain and will become one of the most important parts of the entire piece.

## PRO TIPS

- Use gloves to protect your hands from splinters and stain. Sometimes, gloves help with the blending process, too.

- I keep the vibrancy in my boards because I put the lightest colors down first. The only exception to this rule is with White Ning, as I use that more as an accent on top of other colors. I have found that large areas of white don't always have the results I expect so I typically don't use the White Ning for that purpose. But it makes a stunning accent.

**14.** Add Dragon's Belly to the bottom of your piece. I have again placed the stain and added water to it.

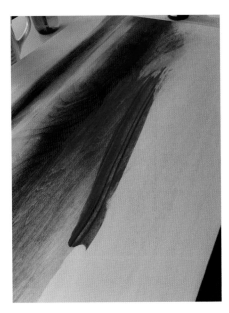

**15.** Navajo Jewel is being blended into the edges of the Dragon's Belly. Add a significant amount so you have a lot to play with to get the blending just right.

**16.** Use Navajo Jewel to cover the small strip of darker grain between the two light colors, Zia and Lemon Kiss, at the top of the board. The amount I put down is probably excessive, which means I might end up with a darker top than I initially intended, but I'm thinking it will be a better contrast.

## PRO TIP

- On occasion, I find a little glitch in the wood. Sometimes I get nicks like this where the sanding pulled up a little chunk, and sometimes, I actually find wormholes! Wood will always have imperfections. The fun part for me is to try and see how I can work with them. In this case, it was a pretty glaring nick, so I opted to just fill it in. The easiest way to fill in these deep nicks is to take a pointed cotton swab and dip it in the stain and then push it into the nick.

17. **NOTE:** This is my signature effect that I strive for in most of my paintings. I love how the blended, pulled stain can become such an interesting focal point.

18. Drag a big line of Dragon's Belly Green across the bottom. You can always go over parts of it to bring out the accent detail you need.

19. Add Midnight's Blackness but start with a small amount. Actually, I believe I used the concept color, Hades. As usual, just use a small amount. Less is always more with Unicorn SPiT.

# CHAPTER THREE

# Glass

Habitat for Humanity ReStore is one of my favorite places to visit. You can find old windows, outdated chandeliers, lampshades, and every once in a while, you'll come across vases and old serviceware. I find that the clear glass that's considered outdated makes the perfect canvas for Unicorn SPiT. You can turn it into blown glass, stained glass, or even carnival glass (glass with an iridescent glaze). You're going to be so inspired when you see glass from now on.

# Marbled Vase

### What you'll need

- Unicorn SPiT colors: Blue Thunder, Purple Hill Majesty, Zia, and Dragon's Belly
- Concept color: Zeus
- E6000 Spray Adhesive
- Water
- Five plastic cups
- Clean and prepared glass vase
- Syringe

Clear glass vases are common; they're nearly at every yard sale I visit. Thrift store shelves are chock-full of them. When I receive flowers, they usually come in a clear glass vase as well. They are so prevalent that people discard them. I couldn't be happier about this because vases have become the perfect canvas to express my fluid art. I love to watch the colors cascade down the sides, creating a look of carved or turned elaborate stones. The color combinations are endless, and they can easily fit into your decor. Whether you showcase them with or without flowers, they turn out so pretty.

# Directions

1. Start by mixing your colors. Mix 1 part Unicorn SPiT to 4 parts E6000 Spray Adhesive. Add a splash of water until you get a runny, warm honey like consistency.

2. Set your vase upside down on top of a wine bottle so the bottom of the vase does not touch your work surface. Make sure that your table is level and start pouring your different colors on top of the vase in any order you desire.

3. If you feel that your colors are getting a little monotonous or you want to add an extra splash of color to a certain area, you can fill up a syringe. As you can see in the photo, I have Zia and concept color Zeus gold in the syringe.

4. As opposed to pouring the paint in the middle, as you did with the other colors, a syringe allows you to place color just where you want it.

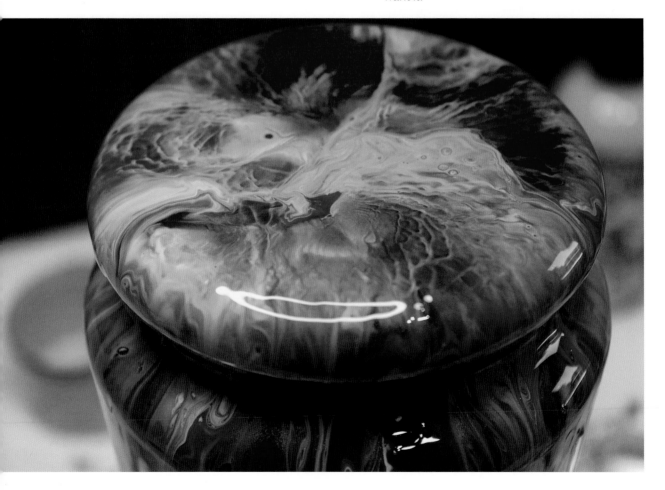

**5.** After your vase is covered to your desire, whisp a flame across the wet surface, popping any bubbles. Be careful not to overheat as you do not want to boil the medium or stress the glass, which might make it crack. Allow the vase to dry for at least 12 hours.

**6.** When your design is dry, use 220-grit sandpaper on the upper brim of the vase to give it a nice, clean look. There is no need to further seal it if you plan to use this vase for dry arrangements or dry storage. It will dry to a matte finish. Feel free to seal the vase with an oil-based topcoat of your choice if you plan to use this for wet arrangements. The design will not be 100-percent waterproof unless you seal it with epoxy.

## PRO TIPS

- You can do this design on the interior or exterior of the glass. Putting the glass on a cuptisserie turner with epoxy makes it look like a real glass-blown vase.
- Don't worry about covering the entire surface; letting some areas stay translucent allows for further creativity. By spray painting the interior gold or silver, you'll create a mirror or metallic peek-a-boo effect.

# Seasonal Glass Shade

## What you'll need

- Unicorn SPiT colors: Phoenix Fire, Lemon Kiss, and White Ning
- Artist brushes
- Glass shades
- Paint palette

As I've said many times, Unicorn SPiT doesn't have to be sealed. If it's not going to be handled often or exposed directly to water, it can be dry Unicorn SPiTTED, which makes it easy to change the item with the seasons. All you need is to give the piece a simple rinse of water and a light scrub.

For this project, I will show you how I paint my glass shades (globes) over my kitchen island to fit every season. It doesn't matter if the glass is clear or frosted for you to be able to set the mood for any time of year. I'm going to show you how to make candy corn shades that are perfect for fall.

# Directions

1. Remove the shade from the light fixture, clean, dry, then place on a Lazy Susan so you can easily twirl it.

2. To create the candy corn look, alternate stripes of Phoenix Fire, White Ning, and Lemon Kiss. Apply Unicorn SPiT in full strength with no dilution.

3. It's easy to center your shade on the Lazy Susan to paint perfect stripes all the way around by spinning it while your brush touches the surface.

4. Once dry, reattach the shade to the light fixture.

5. When you're ready for a change of season, remove the shade from the light fixture and wash it with water and a scrub brush. Allow it to dry and create another design.

## PRO TIPS

- To make the design permanent, seal the piece with an oil-based, brush-on or spray topcoat. I do not recommend finishing wax or salve.

- If the glass is resisting the SPiT, spray shades with frosted glass spray to give the surface some tooth.

- If you don't want to paint your existing shades, glass shades can be found at thrift stores.

- If the color doesn't completely disappear when washing off, you can clean the shades with a Magic Eraser after removing the majority of the color.

# Faux Leaded Stained-Glass Owl

Single-paned windows with wood frames are no longer energy efficient, so the trend has moved to double-paned windows that have a vapor barrier. As a result, the old windows are being tossed into the trash. When I was in survival mode after I left the day care, I came across a construction site with discarded windows. I pulled over and asked the workers if I could have the old windows. To my delight, they were happy to load them up for me because then they didn't have to pay to drop them at the dump. Getting a truckload of single-paned windows meant groceries for the week. I sold the windows, as is, to people making farmhouse decor and turning them into photo collage frames for their walls.

When I was young, my mom painted the sidelights in my childhood home with glass paint from the '80s and made them look like stained glass. I was always fascinated by them. I thought about the sidelights and decided to see if I could somehow make Unicorn SPiT work like those expensive glass paints. I can honestly say that the process I discovered was more durable and more realistic-looking than any other glass painting technique I have ever seen. I'm sure you'll be pulling over on the side of the road or going to ReStore to pick up those single-paned windows. Why not have multicolored rays of light beam into your home and flow through the art you create?

## What you'll need

- Unicorn SPiT colors: Zia, Blue Thunder, and Purple Hill Majesty
- Concept colors: Zeus and Athena
- Single-paned window
- Permanent marker
- Outlined image on a transparency sheet
- Overhead projector (if you don't have one, print image to scale)
- Liquid leading
- Super glue
- Razor blade
- Razor blade paint scraper
- Glass accent gems
- FAMOWOOD Glaze Coat
- Spray bottle of water
- Rubbing alcohol
- Shop cloth
- DiY Alcohol iNKS in white, gold, pink, and purple (see page 13)

## Directions

1. Prepare the glass by cleaning it thoroughly.

2. Line the glass with white paper so the projector can beam the image onto the glass to trace easily.

3. Project the image and adjust it to fit the glass. Trace the image with your permanent marker.

4. Lay your window with the image on a level surface, with the marker side down. Remove the paper and trace the marker lines with the liquid leading. Allow the liquid leading to cure.

**5.** Flip the glass over with the leading side down and remove the marker lines easily with a cloth and rubbing alcohol.

**6.** Glue glass gems on the side without the liquid leading. You will be doing all of your art on the clean side, using the opposite side with liquid leading as your guide.

**7.** Apply small dollops of Purple Hill Majesty and Blue Thunder in the first section you color. Then use a brush to blend the colors using downward stroke motions to emulate the flow of feathers.

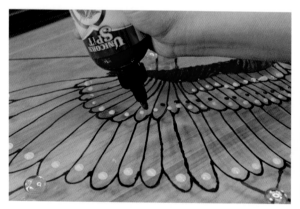

**8.** I use small dots of Zia at the end of the feathers, with Blue Thunder above them. Apply Purple Hill at the top of the last layer of feathers to create depth. Purple Hill Majesty will be the darkest tone.

**9.** Add dollops of Blue Thunder to the edges of the owl's torso, and Zia in the middle of his torso to create depth.

**10.** Drag a wide, soft bristle brush through the colors. Starting with the bottom layer of feathers first, work upward, using gentle brushstrokes that become lighter at the end for a soft, airy look. Continue these steps for the tail and the top of his head as well.

**11.** Do the same for his torso, keeping the lightest tone in the middle and the darkest on the side, fading to his feet.

**12.** If it looks too streaky and you feel that you want it to be more translucent, mist it with water and allow it to dry.

**13.** Once dry, put your projector light under the window to clean up any colorant that may have flowed outside of the lines. You can use the razor blade paint scraper to clean up large areas of color.

**14.** Use a pencil eraser to clean up the colorant and expose the black lines. You will be putting leading on this side as well and you want it to line up.

**15.** To make the halo around the owl, drip your Unicorn SPiT Alcohol iNKS in random droplets to fill in the halo ring. Allow it to dry and clean up with the razor blade and/or eraser.

## PRO TIP

· You can use brushstrokes to create a textured look.

**16.** Use undiluted Zeus in an alcohol ink bottle to apply the colorant to tight detail areas like the claws, beak, eyes, and arrow.

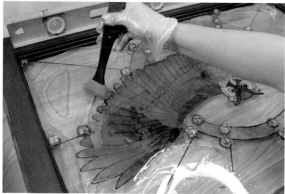

**17.** When it's fully dried and you are pleased with the look, you are ready to seal. Pour on the epoxy. Make sure you spread it from edge to edge, all the way to the frame.

## PRO TIP

· Unicorn SPiT is going to dry chalky and look as if it's lost its vibrant color. Remember how it looked when it was wet, to gauge whether you should seal it or not. Once you seal it, all the intensity of color will come back.

**18.** If you want to add dimension, you can drip your METALLiC gold Alcohol iNK onto the uncured epoxy to create beautiful gold ringlets.

## PRO TIP

- Lightly and swiftly apply a flame to the epoxy once it's poured to remove bubbles or to leave bubbles for a seeded glass look.

**19.** If you drip Alcohol iNK into the wet epoxy, it will look as though the coloring is denting the epoxy, but it will self-level. The color rings will be smooth and expand to look as though these magical golden prisms are within the glass. Allow it to cure and, if desired, trace the pattern on the epoxied side with leading. Now it's ready to hang.

# Carnival Glass Trinket Holder

## What you'll need

- SPARKLiNG Unicorn SPiT colors: Lavish Lovebirds, Sapphire Swift, Dolly Firebird, and Golden Gosling
- Glass container
- Clear frosted glass aerosol spray
- High-gloss spray (optional)
- Medium-sized brush
- Straw
- Spray bottle of water
- Shop cloth

Carnival glass and blown glass have always caught my attention. Honestly, I wish all glass was that, especially the glass serviceware I inherited from family members. I can't say this is going to be an exact replica of carnival glass, but it definitely satisfies my desire for its multifaceted allure.

# Directions

1. Clean the glass with clear frosted glass aerosol spray on all of the areas where you want to add color and allow it to dry.

2. Paint the entire surface with Sapphire Swift.

3. Add drops of other colors over the top of the blue and use the straw to blow the colors around. You can follow a pattern or just go with it.

4. You will notice that the SPARKLiNG Unicorn SPiT might look lumpy, but that's okay.

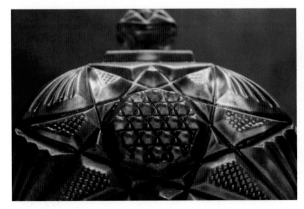

5. As you can see, once it's dry, it all self-levels and the little lumps disappear. You know that it's dry and ready to be sealed when it's no longer shiny and has a matte or a satin finish.

6. With a wet shop cloth, wipe away any areas you do not want the SPARKLiNG Unicorn SPiT, such as on the rim.

**7.** Seal with frosted glass aerosol spray or a high-gloss spray for a true carnival glass look.

## PRO TIPS

- The frosted aerosol spray gives the Unicorn SPiT SPARKLiNG more tooth to stick to, but you may need to apply two coats of the base color to get full coverage.

- If you don't have a frosted glass spray handy, you can also use glass etching cream.

- Don't be afraid to highlight with a little metallic color, like copper, of your choice if desired.

- If you don't like how it looks, simply wash it off with water before sealing.

# Chandelier

I am the mother of sons, but I have always wanted a little girl. My desire to make a room filled with whimsical, girly, and fairytale decor hasn't gone away. I could just imagine having this discarded and outdated chandelier as the showpiece crowning the whole room. You can go to just about any ReStore and find these 1990s glass-paned two- and three-tiered chandeliers. I have discovered a way to mix Unicorn SPiT with household rubbing alcohol and drip it on the glass panes to resemble handblown Favrile art glass. This kaleidoscope of color looks beautiful in a lit room but looks even more beautiful when it illuminates a darkened room as a prism of color dances across the walls. This project will surely get all of the 1990s glass chandeliers off the shelves and into imagination-inspired homes.

## What you'll need

- Make the following colors into Alcohol iNKS (see page 13). Unicorn SPiT colors you will use to make the ink: Pixie Punk Pink, Blue Thunder, and Dragon's Belly
- Concept color: Zeus
- Embossing heat tool
- High-gloss aerosol spray
- Shop cloth
- Spray bottle of water
- Glass cleaner
- Super cheesy, outdated, multi-tiered, glass-paned chandelier

# Directions

1. After thoroughly cleaning the glass, place the glass front-side down on top of a white surface. This will help you better see the colors as you apply them. Make sure they are face-side down and that the tops and bottoms are lined up in the same direction.

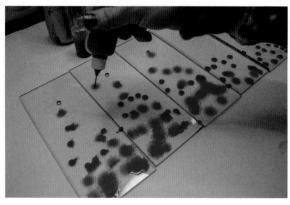

2. Starting at the bottom, begin by dripping the pink Alcohol iNK. Work your way up in a triangle pattern on each panel.

3. Apply the blue toward the middle, creating a diamond pattern per panel, and working your way to the top and then down.

4. Apply the blue sporadically over the pink and enjoy that little bit of magic that happens. You'll love it.

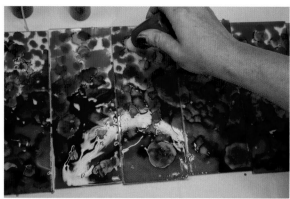

5. Now, drip the green on the top of each panel. Feel free to drip a little of the green over the blue in that same downward, triangle pattern.

**6.** Using your gold metallic, add small, sporadic drops here and there, on the top, bottom, and middle of each pattern. Let it dry.

**7.** If there are any areas with bare glass, feel free to fill them in with any colors you feel will look best in that area. Let that dry.

**8.** I felt that the gold we applied wasn't as prevalent as I wanted it to be, so I dripped additional gold over the dried Alcohol iNKS to make it more prominent. I let that dry.

**9.** Lay your glass out and seal with a high-gloss oil-based topcoat, preferably an aerosol. Use two or three coats, allowing each coat to dry in between.

**10.** With a wet shop towel, remove excess iNK from the front of each panel that may have leaked from the back.

## PRO TIP

· To speed up drying, you can use an embossing tool, a hair dryer, or a heat gun.

11. Use a wet cloth to clean up the edges. If the topcoat sealed the edges, carefully take a razor blade paint scraper or 220-grit sandpaper and scrape it off. This gives each panel a nice, clean, professional look.

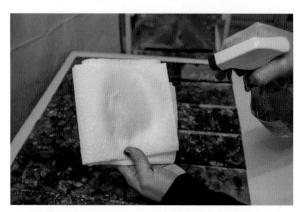

12. Spray a paper towel with window cleaner and polish the front side of the glass. It's very important to spray the paper towel with the glass cleaner as opposed to spraying the glass with the cleaner. You wouldn't want to have the glass cleaner lift your artwork if it's not 100-percent sealed. It's best to play it safe. Now you're ready to install them on your previously cheesy chandelier that is now a work of art.

# CHAPTER FOUR

# Metal

You can SPiT iron, aluminum, brass, tin, or whatever metal artifact you have. There are unlimited possibilities so don't shy away from metal objects that are rusted and corroded—that just gives it texture. One day, one of our SPiTTERs walked by his truck, saw his shiny grill and thought, "I can SPiT that." And he did. There's no limit to what you can add color to, but the key will be prepping and sealing. So, don't let the semi-nonporus elements of metal deter you from your colorful adventures (see preparing metal on page 2).

# Metal Garden Flower

### You will need

- Unicorn SPiT colors: Lemon Kiss and Pixie Punk Pink
- Large metal flower
- Jumbo-sized flat brush

Currently, the farmhouse look is all the rage. Everywhere you go you see primitively cut-metal decor. While I enjoyed it for a while, I found that I constantly imagined what color the metal could be rather than its robot-looking state. I wanted to give it some life, so I decided that it should glow with the beautiful colors of Dahlias. Now, this flower brightens my garden and my day every time I see it.

# Directions

1. Apply a drop of Lemon Kiss on the base of each petal.

2. Use your dry jumbo brush to grab a drop of color and pull it outward, covering each petal.

3. Use your brush to wiggle the color into all crevices and let it dry.

4. Make a pile of Pixie Punk Pink to dip your brush into. Lightly graze your brush across the tip of each petal, pulling inward with very light strokes.

5. Continue grazing each of the petals, using the little hairs of your brush to create realistic color variegation on your petals. Don't be afraid to turn your brush from flat to narrow to get more intricate, concentrating the majority of the color on the outside.

6. Let it dry. If it's going to be for interior use, you don't need to seal it, as the color won't flake or fall off on its own. For added durability or exterior use, seal with your preferred interior or exterior topcoat in matte, satin, or gloss. It's up to you.

## PRO TIPS

- I suggest searching online for different variegated-colored flowers and choose your colors. I like to start with the light color first, always moving to the darker tone.
- If you don't want your colors to blend together, seal between colors.

# Rainbow Pride Tiara

Plain silver metal tiaras are everywhere. If you want something elaborate or colorful, you're usually stuck with something plastic. No royalty should settle for a plastic tiara with colorful plastic gems. Upgrade your royal status and take pride in this beautiful rainbow tiara that will celebrate your diva desires.

## What you'll need

- Unicorn SPiT colors: Sapphire Swift, Golden Gosling, and Dolly Firebird
- Tiara
- Eyeshadow sponge or soft cloth
- Paintbrush
- Hair spray

# Directions

1. Start with a clean piece of costume jewelry like this tiara pictured.

2. Use a paintbrush to paint a horizontal stripe of Dolly Firebird across the tiara in two different areas.

3. Make a horizontal stripe of Golden Gosling. Let the Dolly Firebird and the Golden Gosling mix where they meet to create an orange color.

4. Add a horizontal stripe of Sapphire Swift. Allow it to mix where it meets the Dolly Firebird to create purple.

5. Top off with Golden Gosling where it meets the Sapphire Swift to create green.

## PRO TIPS

- Apply the SPiT so it can go behind the stones.
- I prefer to use SPARKLiNG Unicorn SPiT because it's more translucent than Unicorn SPiT.
- If you decide to change the color, you'll be able to rinse off the color with water.
- You can make the color permanent with a spritz of a topcoat.

6. After it's dry, use a damp makeup sponge to polish the front of the stones and to remove any excess.

7. Seal with hair spray.

# Stain Press Tumbler

## What you'll need

- Unicorn SPiT colors: SQUiRREL, Phoenix Fire, and White Ning
- SPARKLiNG colors: Golden Gosling and Starling Sasha
- Metal tumbler of your choice
- Epoxy, like FAMOWOOD Glaze Coat
- Cuptisserie
- Clear plastic wrap
- Electrical tape
- Disposable gloves
- Torch
- Acetone
- Shop cloth

People are becoming eco-conscious and shying away from disposable plastic cups, straws, and bottles. Instead, they're migrating to refillable cups that insulate and keep your beverage hot or cold. While there are many designs on the market with different mass-produced art on them, what's better than carrying around a personalized tumbler to express your eco-friendly ideals? For this project, I will show you how to use my signature stain-press technique on a metal tumbler embellished with stickers. Then it's sealed to become waterproof, durable, and an eco-friendly fashion accessory. Don't be surprised if your friends ask you to make one for them.

# Directions:

1. Starting with a clean cup, use electrical tape to block off any area that you don't want the epoxy to touch (such as the area where your mouth comes into contact with the cup). Start SPiTTiNG about ¼ of an inch down from the rim. You will need this blank band of metal when it comes to epoxy. I like to use electrical tape on the space because you can pull it, stretch it, and make it really tight. It bonds well to metal. Make sure you make a straight line with your tape, so it has a nice clean look.

## PRO TIPS

- You can add multiple layers of the tape if needed. I generally add about two or three.

- You can use any colors you desire to create different color combos, but I do recommend using colors that will blend well. Look at the color wheel for ideas (see page 3).

- You can use colored tumblers; they don't have to be plain metal. You can do full coverage or use the color of the tumbler to peek through for added interest.

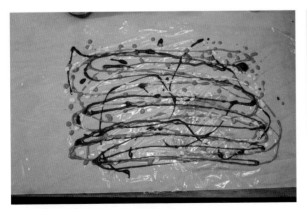

2. Lay out a piece of clear plastic wrap large enough to go around your cup. Lay the wrap flat on the table and apply drips and drizzles of all the colors all over it. Make sure to use a lot of White Ning for contrast.

3. Place your tumbler on a detached cuptisserie-turning bracket to act as a handle. Put one hand on the plastic wrap to secure it to the table. Put your cup on the collage of colors, starting at the end closest to your other hand.

**4.** Start rolling your cup across the colors.

**5.** You can spin gradually while you roll, to intensify the colors smearing on your cup.

**6.** You can repeat the same spinning and rolling process if you need to cover missing spots or you want to blend the color more.

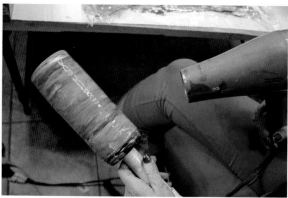

**7.** Let it dry, then remove the tape. Because Unicorn SPiT doesn't contain plastic, when you remove the tape, even when it's dry, you'll have nice, clean, sharp lines.

**8.** If you want to add more flare to your cup, such as transfers, stickers, or vinyl, seal using a clear aerosol topcoat. It doesn't matter if it's high gloss or matte. Whatever you have on hand, two coats are advised, allowing each coat to cure between applications.

**9.** Now that the spray topcoat is dry, you can add your embellishments.

10. Once your cup is embellished the way you like, connect it to your cuptisserie, turn it on to start turning and apply your epoxy.

## PRO TIP

- I absolutely love stickers from dollar stores. When using the stiff ones, it's good to bend them before you apply them so they don't flatten out. Feel free to print out your own waterslide images or use temporary tattoos.

11. Use your gloved hand to smooth the epoxy over the entire tumbler sides and bottom, working the epoxy up to the finish line where you removed the tape. Go over the top band of metal but stop at the point where it might interfere with the lid mechanism.

12. Quickly pass a flame across the epoxy, popping any bubbles, but be careful not to overheat or boil. You only want to pop the bubbles.

13. If you happen to go over the area where the lid screws on, there's no need to panic. You can wipe this off easily using acetone or rubbing alcohol. Use a shop towel instead of cotton to keep any loose fibers from getting on your epoxy.

14. Allow your cup to cure while turning on the cuptisserie for at least 12 hours. Once it's dry, it's ready to remove and use.

# Gaming Zone Metal Sign

## What you'll need

### For Dip

- Unicorn SPiT colors: Lemon Kiss, Phoenix Fire, and Molly Red Pepper
- Liquid school glue
- Mixing cups
- Stir sticks
- Marker
- Metal sign blank

### For Stenciling

- Midnight's Blackness
- Heavy gel acrylic medium
- Stir stick and palette
- Stencils
- Stencil brush
- Paper towel
- Ruler
- Pencil

I've always been interested in helping those with disabilities and challenges learn to express themselves. I'm proud to share this project by Isaac Stark, a teenager on the autism spectrum with two rare medical conditions. His mother has spent so much time finding ways to make her son shine. You can see by his well-executed work that he is comfortable making art and talented as well.

# Directions

1. Mix 1 part Unicorn SPiT to 3 parts glue. The colors will appear lighter as the glue is white. When it dries, the colors will be vibrant. The consistency should be like warm honey. If needed, add a few drops of distilled or filtered water to get the correct consistency. Let the color mixture rest while you do the next couple of steps.

2. Clean the metal sign with rubbing alcohol. Even though the metal has been coated with a smooth finish, there is no need to sand it or do any other prep.

3. Trace around the sign to ensure you know where to place the paint.

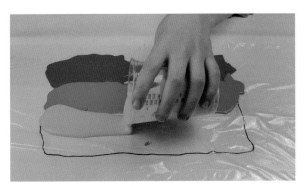

4. Pour the color mixture in rows from darkest to lightest.

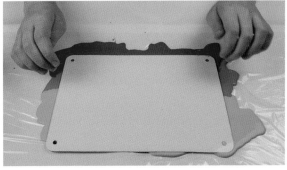

5. Place the metal sign blank facedown on the colors. Gently press down for even coverage. This is called a dip.

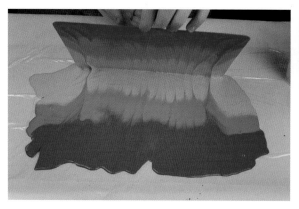

**6.** Carefully and slowly pull up the sign, starting from the darkest color.

**7.** Let it dry overnight.

**8.** If you are not using a stencil with an adhesive backing, mix the Unicorn SPiT with a heavy gel acrylic medium. This will help reduce the amount of bleeding and your project will have crisper lines.

**9.** Position the stencil and measure if necessary. Pencil lines are easily erased after the project is dry. Dip the stencil brush into the mixture, dab off excess onto a paper towel, and stencil using a straight up-and-down movement.

**10.** Let it dry and seal with a clear spray sealer of your choice.

**11.** Tie the rope through the holes to hang.

## PRO TIPS

· When pulling up the piece, don't pull it up too fast or too slow. Use a steady motion.

· If possible, mix your colors 20 minutes or more before you do your project. Cover the colors to prevent them from drying and let them sit. This will reduce the number of bubbles in your colors, providing you with a nicer finished product.

· Don't worry about getting paint on your hands. It will wash off.

# Blinging Belt Buckle

There is nothing cuter than a little girl decked out in cowgirl bling. Here's how I took big brother's hand-me-down belt buckle and made it work for a rodeo princess. Every girl loves to sparkle and with Unicorn SPiT SPARKLiNG, it becomes one with metal's natural shine. You will be surprised at how glossy and beautiful the metal becomes. It will almost look like it was carved out of a gem.

## What you'll need

- Unicorn SPiT SPARKLiNG: Starling Sasha
- Fine-tip brush
- Clean metal belt buckle
- Clear, high-gloss nail polish or UV gel nail topcoat
- Shop cloth

# Directions

**1.** Begin with a pile of Starling Sasha on your palette.

**2.** Apply Starling Sasha liberally to all areas that you want to cover. Let it dry. Then apply a second coat of color for full coverage.

**3.** Wipe away any excess with a wet shop cloth.

**4.** When the Starling Sasha is fully dry, you can seal the buckle using the clear nail polish topcoat of your choice. If you use regular polish, you may want to apply four or five coats, allowing each coat to dry in between. Or if you're using a UV gel nail topcoat, apply two or three coats, exposing the buckle to the UV light in between coats.

## PRO TIPS

- Don't worry if one coat isn't enough. Metal may resist the first coat of SPARKLiNG, but that first dried coat acts as a great primer to build up the depth.
- A UV-cured topcoat works great on an array of surfaces and gives the look of enamel.

# CHAPTER FIVE

# Textiles

Fabric definitely loves Unicorn SPiT, and so do leather and feathers. It doesn't matter if it is natural fiber or synthetic—it makes the perfect canvas to add a splash of color to your fashion and decor. One thing I absolutely love about Unicorn SPiT on textiles is that, unlike a paint that's heavily compacted with plastics, it does not change the texture of the fabric or the way it flows or moves. You won't get that thick, leathery feel. If it wasn't for the color, you wouldn't know it was there at all. It permeates the fabric. You can use Unicorn SPiT for everyday decor in your home. I'm also going to show you how to make it resistant to the elements to create shade or to make an artistic statement every time you put on your shoes.

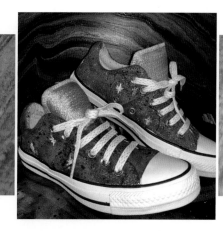

# Sparkling Western Boots

## What you'll need

- SPARKLiNG SPiT: Starling Sasha
- Pair of non-glossy leather, suede, or synthetic-suede boots
- Medium, flat, and a fine-tip artist brush
- Hair dryer
- Hemp sealing salve
- Wax brush

Nothing screams Americana more than a great pair of western boots and a matching belt. The best thing about finding a great pair of western boots or a great leather belt is you don't have to be a ranch hand to show them off. You're going to love the ability to collect various pieces of leather, color them to match, and create your own customized set fit for rodeo royalty. The most wonderful thing about this set I created is the belt. It was a hand-me-down from my oldest boy, and the boots I found at my local thrift store. Luckily, the belt was a souvenir we bought my son when we went to Tombstone, Arizona. I love being able to take memorable items and use them to create new memories. I was able to turn this set of boots and a belt into a set that's girly and sparkly.

# Directions

1. Dip your brush in your SPARKLiNG SPiT and apply it to the clean leather, following the existing stitched-in design. Fill it in like a coloring book. If there is no design, feel free to create your own.

2. Dry the SPiT with your hair dryer set on high heat until completely dry.

3. Load up your wax brush with your sealing salve or clear shoe polish and buff the oils over the color. Make sure you apply generously but not so much that there's a large amount pooling on top. You want it to absorb into the leather. Let the boots cure for 24 hours and they're ready to wear.

NOTE: You can follow these same steps to create a matching belt.

## PRO TIPS

- Make sure the leather is dry when you apply Unicorn SPiT, regular or SPARKLiNG. If using regular Unicorn SPiT, be sure to dilute with water so it can absorb into the leather.

- If the pile on the leather suede seems matted or overly worn, buff the surface using a stiff scrub brush or even a wire brush.

# Galaxy Canvas Shoes

## What you'll need

- Unicorn SPiT colors: White Ning and Midnight's Blackness
- Unicorn SPiT SPARKLiNG: Violet Vulture, Sapphire Swift, and Golden Gosling
- Pair of white canvas shoes
- Medium artist's brush
- Liner brush
- Silicone waterproofing spray for exterior fabrics
- Painter's tape
- Hair dryer
- Cotton makeup remover pad

Trendy footwear is something I really love. I have a ton of shoes, which is crazy because most of the time I'm barefoot. I work out, run around the house, and garden in bare feet. But when I wear shoes, I like them to be ones that express my feelings, mood, and the occasion. I am fascinated with images of outer space, so I took an old pair of white canvas shoes and gave them an out-of-this-world makeover. Don't be afraid to wear these shoes everywhere you go because the way you're going to seal them, they'll be ready to accompany you on your greatest adventures.

# Directions

1. Remove the shoelaces and tape off any areas that you do not wish to color. I chose to cover all the rubber areas as well as the upper area of the tongue because it was glittery and pretty. You do not have to worry about taping off any of the metal.

2. Starting with Violet Vulture, color your galaxy by alternating triangle-like shapes. Start from the bottom up, then the top down, and continue until you get a giraffe-like pattern.

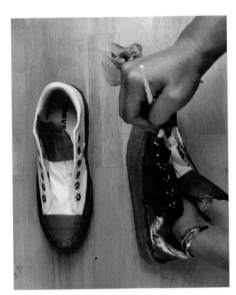

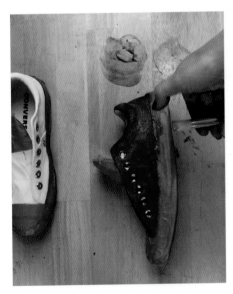

3. Once you have your Violet Vulture down, you can fill in all the gaps using Sapphire Swift. Don't be afraid to allow the colors to overlap. This will create a multitone effect.

4. To create little golden stars, load a stiff brush with some Golden Gosling. Use your thumb to rub against the bristles, allowing the color to flick onto the canvas, here and there. I call this speckling.

**5.** Continue speckling and add some stars using some White Ning. Add some bigger stars by using your liner brush.

**6.** Add asteroids to your galaxy by speckling with Midnight's Blackness.

**7.** Now it's time to heat-set these colors by using a hair dryer on high heat at a minimum of 3 inches away. Dry until the fabric is no longer damp.

**8.** Wet your cotton pad with a little water and easily wipe away excess from any metal areas.

9. After your shoes are fully dried and the metal is cleaned up, you can seal them using exterior fabric silicone waterproofing spray.

10. Remove the tape and if you have any bleeds, clean them up using your damp cotton pad.

## PRO TIPS

- You can also do this on black canvas shoes for an oil-slick look.
- You can water down the SPARKLiNG to get less intense colorization when working on the white canvas.
- Don't be afraid to try the stain press methods as well. You're not limited to galaxies.
- If you don't want your galaxies to sparkle, use regular Unicorn SPiT, but be sure to dilute it with 3–10 parts water.

11. Once the silicone waterproofing spray has completely cured, you can lace up the shoes and they will be ready to go.

# Pop-up Tent

### What you'll need

- Unicorn SPiT in colors: Blue Thunder, Purple Hill Majesty, and Pixie Punk Pink
- Concept color: Zeus
- White and clean pop-up tent
- Four spray bottles
- Water
- Waterproofing silicone spray for exterior fabrics
- Shop cloth

Barbecue competitions, tailgating, and craft shows always have a need for some shade. So instead of blending in with the crowd, here is an exciting way to express your individuality. This pop-up tent surely stands out in a sea of commercial motifs. This is a larger project and one you'll want to do outdoors. Don't hesitate to do smaller items such as umbrellas and even stroller covers. You can get as creative as you want. I decided to let the colors flow all over it.

# Directions

**1.** Set up your pop-up tent. Preferably, do this on a sunny day in the grass because you don't want to stain your concrete. Unicorn SPiT will not harm your grass, so don't worry.

**2.** Squirt your Unicorn SPiT into a spray bottle and dilute with 1 part Unicorn SPiT to 3–10 parts water. I made two bottles of each color. One was extremely diluted and one was less diluted to give a contrast between light and bold coloring.

**3.** After your water and SPiT is in the bottle, put the spray handle back on and shake.

**4.** Mist your canopy with water. You will be misting often to keep the surface wet, especially if it's a hot day.

**5.** Using your spray bottles, mist your colors onto the canvas, allowing them to drip down the edges. Starting at the top seems to work the best to create this colorful drizzle effect.

**6.** After all the colors have flowed to your liking, allow to dry and set your bottle's nozzle to the mist setting. This will let you add softer poofs of color over the bold, drizzled streaks. I chose to spray all the areas that were still white with Zeus to give it a golden, glistening effect.

**7.** At this point, you can stand back, look at it, and decide if you want to add more drizzles, more mists of color, or metallic speckling like I did. If you're pleased with it, move on to the next step. If not, wash it off with a hose and give it another whirl.

**8.** Using a damp shop cloth, you can wipe away any over-spray that may have gotten on the legs or frame. Also, you can easily wipe away colorant that may have covered any logos or images, for a nice, clean look. You can wipe away the color while it's still wet or dry. It doesn't matter. Let it dry.

**9.** After your design has dried, it's time to seal it. Use your silicone waterproof spray that's meant for outdoor fabrics and douse that sucker down. When the waterproofing spray has saturated all the fabric, allow it to dry, following the spray manufacturer's directions.

## PRO TIPS

- When doing a large project like this, be sure not to extend the legs all the way, so you can reach the top without having to use a ladder.

- For this project, I started with very strong bolts of color, setting my spray-bottle nozzle on stream. In hindsight, I would have applied a base color first, using the heavily diluted mix and using the mist setting on the bottle.

- If you would like to customize the tent, you can always add a reverse stencil by applying a custom vinyl stencil or creating words or your business name using painter's tape. If you decide to use vinyl or painter's tape, make sure you burnish it well before applying colors.

# Personalized Pillows

As you might know through following me, one thing that's not in my wheelhouse is sewing. So, if you don't have a friend who can sew, find pillowcases around the house or pick up some blank ones. There's nothing like decorating your living room for the season with cute throw pillows. Follow along with Pam Atteberry as she shows you how to stencil a super-sweet spring design that's machine washable.

## What you'll need

- Unicorn SPiT colors: Lemon Kiss, Dragon's Belly, Purple Hill Majesty, Blue Thunder, and Dolly Firebird
- Concept color: Athena
- E6000 Fabri-Fuse
- Stir sticks
- Small containers to mix above items
- Painters Tape
- Stencil
- A couple of stencil brushes
- Paper plate or palette
- Paper towels
- Water
- Heat source

# Directions

1. In a resealable container, combine 1 part Unicorn SPiT to 3 parts E6000 Fabri-Fuse. Stir ingredients until thoroughly mixed, snap on the lid, and let the mixture sit for about 20 minutes.

2. While the SPiT and E6000 Fabri-Fuse are setting, iron your fabric so there are no creases in it. Line the stencil up on your project and secure it down on the top and one side with painter's tape. I recommend putting something under your project to protect your work area from anything coming through the back of the project.

3. Get a small amount of the SPiT on your stencil brush and tap it on a palette or paper towel. You want just a small amount of SPiT on your brush at a time, otherwise it will not spread evenly and will bleed. Hold the stencil still with one hand and, with your stencil brush, make circular movements to apply the SPiT. You can blend two or more colors to get different effects or a new color mix. A good stencil brush will make a big difference.

4. Be careful not to overlap colors where you don't want them.

**5.** You can carefully lift part of the stencil to check on your progress. Just be careful not to move the tape.

**6.** When finished, let it dry for 24 hours. After this, you need to heat-set your work using an iron or heat press.

**7.** Now you're ready to sew your fabric into a pillow or just about anything. Let your imagination do the work!

## PRO TIPS

- You can mix any colors of Unicorn SPiT or concept colors with E6000 Fabri-Fuse.
- I only use a couple of brushes and just rub the SPiT out of the brush I'm using. My favorite brushes are small round brushes.
- If you have a large area to cover, it sometimes helps to allow some of the SPiT to dry some before adding more colors.
- Blending is a great way to add more colors to your project.

# String Art

## What you'll need

- Unicorn SPiT colors: Purple Hill Majesty, Pixie Punk Pink, and Zia
- Concept colors: Artemis and Atlantis
- Wood blank
- Three small cups
- Tack nails
- White cotton craft thread
- Spray bottle of water
- E6000 Plus
- Paper towels
- Artist brushes
- Colored sola wood flowers
- Hammer
- Syringe

Remember doing string art as a kid? Well, it's rapidly becoming a new crafting trend. All you need is some wood and nails and the key element—string. If you're frugal and have limited space, you don't want to have to store hundreds of different colors of string. There's nothing more frustrating than running out of a color in the middle of a project. With this trick, you will have every color of string you will ever need at your fingertips and will only need to buy white string from now on.

# Directions

1. To make the dye for the string, I mixed Purple Hill Majesty, Pixie Punk Pink, and Zia, each with about 15 parts water.

2. Without unraveling the string, place it on a Styrofoam plate and mist it with water. Using a syringe, suck up one color at a time and apply in a pattern onto the string, allowing the colors to absorb into the fibers. If after applying the dye you feel the colorant is fully absorbed, place it on a paper towel to dry.

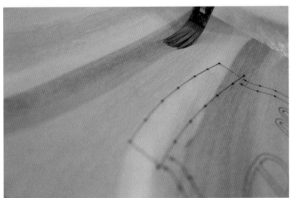

3. Using the same mixture used to dye the thread, you can also stain your board.

4. For the mason jar top design, I decided to color it in with our metallic concept color called Artemis.

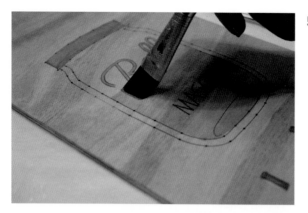

**5.** To enhance the mason jar and make it resemble vintage turquoise glass, I watered down a little of the concept color Atlantis and colored in the jar. I went right over the other colors. I think it's really pretty and added a little bit of luster too.

**6.** It's time to place your nails. This board was great because the placement of the nails was pre-marked.

**7.** Now that your string is dry, it is ready to use.

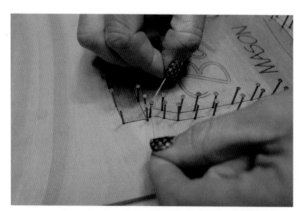

**8.** Tie the end of the string in a knot on the first nail and snip the loose end. It doesn't matter which nail you start with.

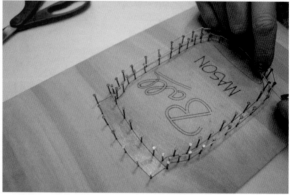

**9.** Now you can have fun taking the string around the head of each nail. Make a loop at the base of the head of the nail and continue onto the next nail until your entire nail pattern is strung together. This will create a multicolored ombre design.

10. Using your sola wood flowers, which you previously colored, put a glob of E6000 Plus on the back of each flower where they're all tied together.

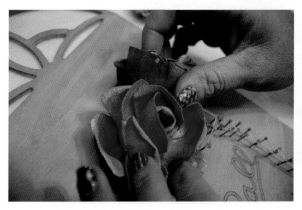

11. Glue each flower to the top of the jar, directly onto the board.

12. Fill in any gap with smaller flowers around the big one for a finished look. Allow it to dry and it's ready to go.

## PRO TIPS

- Mix your colors in resealable jars or plastic storage containers so that you can reuse the diluted SPiT for other projects.
- You can use a hair dryer to dry your string faster.
- If you use yellow, blue, and red, the colors will merge to create a rainbow.
- You can dye any thread—cotton or polyester—for macrame, crocheting, or knitting.
- You can dilute with less water to make the colors bolder.

# Dreamcatcher

## What you'll need

- Unicorn SPiT colors: Navajo Jewel, Midnight's Blackness, White Ning, Zia, Pixie Punk Pink, and Purple Hill Majesty
- Fine-tip artist brushes
- Water
- White dream catcher
- Several plastic cups
- Q-tips

Dreamcatchers have been introduced to homes around the world. They might have mystical powers, but one thing is for sure—they are boho and chic. Of course, you can make this string any color you want by using the process in string art, but what's really neat is you can even color the feathers without compromising their soft, airy, and light texture. When I go shopping for an item I don't already have, I always look for white because I know I can color it to my desire.

# Directions

1. Stretch out your first feather and separate it from the others to work on them one at a time. There's no need to dismantle the dreamcatcher. Make sure you're working on an absorbent surface like dry paper because it will seep through.

**PRO TIP**

· Watercolor paper is super absorbent. Just saying.

2. Begin by dipping your brush into water. Use Zia or the lightest tone and brush onto the feather, starting from the quill, pulling outward to the tips following the flow of the feathers.

3. Apply different colors in a V pattern on both sides from the quill to the tip.

4. Using a fine-tip brush, apply contrasting lines and little dots here and there for dimension.

5. Let it dry.

**6.** Once the feathers are dry, use a wet Q-tip to remove excess from the quill for a nice, clean look.

**7.** Of course, the feathers aren't the only section that is going to get some love. Water down the colors you used to color the feathers. Color the string by painting the watery mix straight onto the crocheted center.

**8.** When it's dry, your colorful dreamcatcher is ready to display.

## PRO TIPS

- The bigger the feather, the more fun you can have with the design.
- Use a fresh piece of paper for every feather. When you pull up the feather, the pattern it leaves behind is so beautiful, you'll want to frame it.

# Upcycled Wedding Dress

They say your wedding dress should only be worn once or handed down to a loved one for their wedding. However, many wedding dresses end up in a thrift store or don't fit the desires of the person you want to hand it down to. Wedding dresses are magical. Think of all the happy feelings they absorb from the person who wore it. So, when I see one at the thrift store, I always snag it. It doesn't matter if it's stained because you will be staining them in color and giving them a brand-new life to bring joy once again.

## What you'll need

- Unicorn SPiT in your choice of colors
- Painter's tape
- Spray bottle of water
- Fabric steamer

# Directions

1. Tape off the fancy embellishments.

2. Dilute Unicorn SPiT, 3 parts water to 1 part SPiT.

3. Spray Unicorn SPiT on the dress and use your gloved hands to blend the colors. Keep a spray bottle of water handy to keep your Unicorn SPiT moveable, blendable, and slick.

5. Let the dress dry, then rinse it with water. Allow it to dry again.

6. Once dry, stream press the wrinkles. The shimmer of the satin will magically come back. The color will not come off. Dry clean only.

4. Add a bit of Unicorn SPiT to your gloved hand to touch up details.

## PRO TIPS

- If it's a darker dress and you want to have big bright vibrant colors, bleach the fabric.
- If it's a black dress, you will want to add a fabric medium to make the colors show up. I would love to see a black dress done in Unicorn SPiT SPARKLiNG. It could look like an oi-slick rainbow.

# Ombre Lampshade

Just like throw pillows can set the mood, so too can a lampshade. It's really fun and super easy to add a splash of color to a lampshade that would otherwise go unnoticed. It's fun to sprinkle your art here and there throughout your home in the simplest ways. I found this lamp on clearance at a hardware store and its base was so pretty I just knew I had to embellish its shade to turn it into a piece of art.

## What you'll need

- Unicorn SPiT color: Zia
- White lampshade
- Spray bottle of water
- Lazy Susan large enough to hold the lampshade
- Jumbo flat brush
- Spray bottle of water

# Directions

1. Line your Lazy Susan with an absorbent base like paper towels. Put a pile of Zia on your palette and mist with water. You don't want to pre-dilute the color. Instead, you want to be able to dilute as you go to get different strengths of the stain. So, leave some of it not fully dissolved.

2. Place the lampshade upside down on your Lazy Susan. Mist the lampshade with water, making sure that all of the fibers are wet.

3. Wet your brush.

4. Dip your brush into your misted pile, half into the pile and half into the water.

5. Put your brush to the lampshade and turn it, giving a nice strong color to the bottom brim of the lampshade.

**6.** Turn your Lazy Susan to do horizontal stripes above the baseline here and there. Take advantage of the pigment running out on your brush to make fainter and fainter lines as you move upward.

**7.** Place your brush on a shop cloth and mist with water to squeeze out any pigment, because it's time to blend.

**8.** Blend the colors by spinning the Lazy Susan and going over those colors with your wet brush. This will reactivate the pigments and allow you to fade them.

**9.** Continue blending the colors using clean water. You can also add more color by reloading your brush with more SPiT and blending with water again and again. When finished, just allow it to dry on its own. There's no need to seal it as cloth lampshades are dry-dust anyway.

## PRO TIPS

- Pick colors that complement the base.
- Hold the lampshade down when you spin because it won't be heavy enough to keep from tipping over when you're applying color.

# Rainbow Rose

## What you'll need

- Unicorn SPiT colors: Molly Red Pepper, Lemon Kiss, and Blue Thunder
- Three alcohol ink bottles
- Painter's tape

We have all gone to the hobby store looking for flowers that perfectly suit a theme, a color scheme, or a person they're intended for. Even though there are hundreds to choose from, you don't have to look any further than the selection of white. You can make them any solid color you like, but I wanted to make these roses a rainbow of color.

# Directions

1. Make a mixture of 1 part Unicorn SPiT to 5–6 parts water and fill your three alcohol ink bottles, one for each color.

2. Use painter's tape to tape off the stem of the rose.

3. With the petals spread out and facing up, drip the Blue Thunder on the tips of the petal, allowing gravity to pull the color down to the middle.

4. Be sure to leave some areas blank for other colors.

5. As carefully as you can, but not with great precision, drip your Molly Red Pepper onto the bare areas. Only drip on the tips of the petal, which will absorb the color to the base.

6. Be sure to leave a couple of places here and there for your final color: Lemon Kiss. But you can see where the red touched the blue and created a beautiful purple.

7. Drip Lemon Kiss on any vacant spots you find. Don't be afraid to go over the Blue Thunder because that will create a beautiful green. Also, don't hesitate to go over the Molly Red Pepper, because that will create a cheerful orange.

8. Allow the rose to dry.

## PRO TIPS

· After it's dried, if the color is too vibrant and you want more of a pastel look, you can rinse your flower under water or soak in bleach water.

· You can increase the vibrancy of the rose by not diluting the color much, or you can dilute it more for a pastel look.

· Spray your roses with silicone waterproofing spray for outdoor display.

# CHAPTER SIX

# Paper and Canvas

Unicorn SPiT can be applied to elaborate surfaces, but when it comes down to basics like water-color paper, canvas, stretched canvas, or mixed media on wood canvas, we've got that covered too. There's no need to buy oil paints or inks or expensive tubes of watercolor. All you need is Unicorn SPiT, a little water, and our unique Pinch Powder Insert (see Resource Guide). If you have the desire to try watercoloring or oil painting, this is a great way to experiment. We're finding that experienced watercolor and oil paint artists prefer to use Unicorn SPiT.

The world needs
*more of you*

# Watercolor Painting

## What you'll need

- Unicorn SPiT Colors: Lemon Kiss, Dragon's Belly, Phoenix Fire, Zia
- Concept colors: Selene and Hades
- Palette
- Small watercolor brushes
- Watercolor paper
- Design
- Water
- Black marker
- Ink
- Stamps

You can use Unicorn SPiT in place of traditional watercolors. Whether the Unicorn SPiT is dried or liquid, you will find that you will utilize a lot more water and a lot less product than you would any other watercolor product on the market today. The tiniest bit will go such a long way, you will be able to watercolor all day. Follow along with Pam Atteberry as she shows you how she created this adorable bumblebee using her favorite watercolor medium, Unicorn SPiT.

# Directions

1. Put small amounts of Unicorn SPiT in a water-color palette container.

2. Allow it to dry. Then choose your design and transfer it to your watercolor paper. You will want to layer your SPiT. I like to start at the top of the design and work my way down the page. Be sure to leave areas very light so that it seems as though the light is hitting them. Darker areas are best made by layering with layers of light to-dark colors.

3. Use Lemon Kiss for the yellow on the top of the flower, a bit of Phoenix Fire for the shadow, and concept color Selene for the highlights. The flower petals are painted with Unicorn SPiT Zia and a little bit of Lemon Kiss. The tips of the petals are highlighted with concept color Selene. The stem is Dragon's Belly lightened up with Unicorn SPiT Lemon Kiss.

# PRO TIPS

- Trace or draw the design very lightly with a pencil so that it doesn't show through when painting.
- Layers work much better than being heavy-handed with the SPiT.
- Good-quality watercolor paper helps a lot.

**Notes about the colors I used:** The bee's body is Lemon Kiss and the highlights are concept color Selene. I used a bit of the Unicorn SPiT Phoenix Fire with a bit of the Lemon Kiss to tone it down a bit for the shadowing of the bee's head and other areas.

The wings are concept color Selene with a bit of Unicorn SPiT. The black stripes and the antennae are painted with concept color Hades.

The wings are painted with concept color Selene with a bit of the Unicorn SPiT Zia for shadowing.

**4.** Once your image is dry, take a black marker and draw around the image to finish it off. I added the eyes, nose, and mouth, then cut the paper into the size I wanted and added a stamped image.

**NOTE:** I made my own SPiT ink with an old ink pad, some Unicorn SPiT Midnight's Blackness, and a small amount of water.

# Fantasy Falls Faux Oil Painting

## What you'll need

- Unicorn SPiT (see next page for colors)
- Black Gesso
- One-inch brush
- Two-inch brush
- Foliage brush
- Fan brush
- Liner brush
- Soft blender brush
- PiNCH Powder
- Mesh wire
- Paper towels

The deep colors, texture, and the art of oil painting sets Unicorn SPiT apart from most mediums because it truly looks amazing. Not only are tubes of oil paint expensive, but they can take months and months to fully dry. I've discovered a way to thicken Unicorn SPiT so that it can be used in place of oil paint. It allows you to use the same tools and techniques for a fraction of the cost, requires as few as 24 hours of drying time, and doesn't sacrifice the look, feel, and intensity of true oil painting. Follow along with our junior artist Haley Sellmeyer as she shows you how she creates a three-dimensional effect using oil painting techniques.

To create a Unicorn SPiT Paint Palette that mimics an oil-paint palette, follow the directions below.

### Faux (oil paint alternative)

1. Mix 1 oz. Sap Green (see pages 11 and 12 for the color mix recipe), two scoops of PiNCH POWDER, and 5 ml palette wetting spray together.

2. If it is not the equivalent to the consistency of oil paint, add a splash of water.

3. Scrape the edges and push down inside the container. Place the lid on it to seal and let it develop for 20 minutes.

Load your palette with Unicorn SPiT colors Midnight's Blackness, Purple Hill Majesty, Blue Thunder, Navajo Jewel, Dragon's Belly, concept color Roswell, Pixie Punk Pink, White Ning, and custom-mixed color Sap Green.

**Concept colors:** Atlantis and Zeus

# Directions

1. Mix 1 oz. of Unicorn SPiT to three scoops of PiNCH POWDER, with 5 ml of palette wetting spray. Let the mixture sit for 20 minutes. Once it's developed, stir until the consistency of the mixture thickens to that of oil paint.

2. Apply Black Gesso to the entire canvas as a basecoat, then let it dry.

3. Load a 2-inch brush with Blue Thunder. Apply a thin undercoat layer of Blue Thunder on ¾ of the canvas (as pictured), working the paint into the canvas.

# PRO TIPS

**These warm colors may need less PiNCH Powder:**

- **Unicorn SPiT colors:** Lemon Kiss, Molly Red Pepper, Pixie Punk Pink, Phoenix Fire, SQUiRREL, Rustic Reality, and White Ning
- **Concept colors:** Athena Copper, Aphrodite Rose Gold, Zeus Gold, and Hephaestus. For these colors, I usually use 2 scoops of PiNCH Powder.

**These cool colors may need more PiNCH Powder:**

- **Unicorn SPiT colors:** Dragon's Belly Green, Blue Thunder, Zia, Navajo Jewel, Purple Hill Majesty, and Midnight's Blackness
- **Concept colors:** Artemis, Poseidon, Atlantis, Oceanus, and DiONYSUS

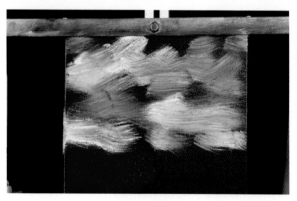

**4.** Clean the 2-inch brush in water, beating the bristles on a mesh wire, then semi-dry with a paper towel.

**5.** Using a foliage brush, make clouds with White Ning by making crisscross motions in the sky. Clean the foliage brush with water, then blend the sky. You can add more Blue Thunder in the sky afterward if desired.

**6.** Use a soft blender brush on the sky by gently swiping back and forth.

**7.** Add additional Blue Thunder to the sky and blend out.

**8.** Use White Ning and your finger to create a moon using a circular motion.

**9.** Load a 2-inch brush with White Ning to create the waterfall by swiping straight down with the flat side of the brush. Add extra color if desired.

**10.** Use a 1- or 2-inch brush loaded with White Ning and make side-to-side motions below the waterfall and to the right, stopping just over halfway to create a river.

11. Use a foliage brush and White Ning to tap lightly, and then make small circular motions to create mist around the waterfall.

12. Use a foliage brush to tap around the bottom of the waterfall to create water splashes.

13. Load a 1-inch brush with Dragon's Belly to make the foundation of the land by tapping in a diagonal line, making different hills, and leaving some black showing through for the shadows. Clean the brush with water.

14. With a 1-inch brush and concept color Roswell, lightly tap into the grassy area to add highlights to the land. Clean the brush with water.

15. With a 1-inch brush and Sap Green, lightly tap into the grassy area to add shadows.

16. With a 1-inch brush, working from the top down, create flowers on the land by tapping in the grassy area with Pixie Punk Pink, Purple Hill Majesty, Blue Thunder, and Navajo Jewel (other colors are optional).

NOTE: Be careful not to overpower the landscape with flowers. Leave space for the grassy area and shadows to show through.

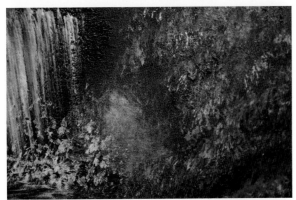

17. Use a fan brush and Midnight's Blackness to make tree trunks. Starting at the top, work your way down to a little over halfway, making the tree trunks thicker at the bottom. Make two tree trunks, leaning in opposite directions.

18. Using a fan brush, mix Midnight's Blackness and White Ning to make a medium gray. Add highlights to the tree trunks with the gray on the side that is closest to the light source. Clean the brush.

19. Using a liner brush with watered-down Midnight's Blackness, make thin branches on the tree by moving the brush from the tree trunk out and up.

20. Load a 1-inch brush with Dragon's Belly, tapping little areas near the branches of the trees to create patches of leaves. Do not clean the brush. Repeat with Sap Green to create an undertone. Using the clean brush, repeat the process with Lemon Kiss and concept color Roswell to add highlights to the leaves. **Optional:** Use a 1-inch brush, add Zeus, and repeat the process to add a mystical feel.

21. **Optional:** Mist the painting with a light spray of water. Then using a fan brush, add additional colors (any you want) in the sky or water to give it a mystical feel.

## PRO TIP

- To save the leftover paint, scrape the paint from the palette into containers and seal with a lid.

# 3-D Paper Bag Stars

This project is fun for a family, large group gatherings, or if you just want to make something for yourself. It's so inexpensive that you can make a whole lot of them for pennies. You can color them for the season, hang them all year long, and easily fold them up to store. Whether you're decorating for a birthday party or holiday party or just feeling a bit festive, these paper bag stars are a showstopper.

## What you'll need

- Unicorn SPiT colors: Navajo Jewel and Purple Hill Majesty
- SPARKLiNG SPiT color: Golden Gosling
- White paper lunch bags
- Three little cups
- Glue stick
- Glue gun
- Ornament hooks
- Scissors
- Plastic covering
- Shop cloth
- Spray bottle of water
- Heat gun or flame

127

# Directions

1. Line up seven lunch bags on a plastic-covered workspace.

2. To make watercolor, drop 5 parts water to 1 part Unicorn SPiT in three separate cups, using Navajo Jewel, Purple Hill Majesty, and Golden Gosling.

3. Brush Navajo Jewel on the front, back, and sides of each bag and line them up again.

4. While the Navajo Jewel is still wet, drip Purple Hill Majesty this way and that. Don't forget the sides.

5. Flip the bags over and splash again with Navajo Jewel.

6. Use Golden Gosling to add another splash of color on both sides.

7. Heat your oven to 200 degrees Fahrenheit. Lay the bags flat on the racks and keep them separated. In 20 minutes, you'll have colorful paper bags. Make sure you keep your eye on the oven while the bags are drying.

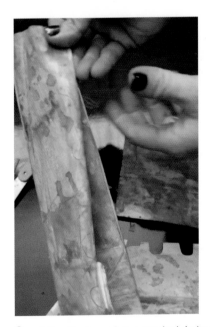

8. While your bags are drying, clean off the colorful puddles from your work surface. All you need is the water in your spray bottle.

9. After the bags have cooled, bring them back to your work surface and fold them in half.

**10.** Cut little circles and a scalloped edge.

**11.** Line each bag up to make a stencil.

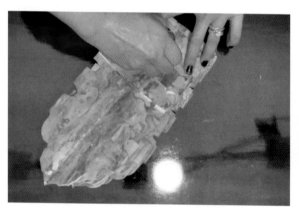

**12.** Now that they're all cut, it's time to glue them together using a glue stick. Apply glue under the flaps to hold them down. Add glue across the bottom, then up the center to the crown. As you glue each one, stack them from bottom to top.

**13.** With water and a wet cloth nearby, allow your paper edges to crisp using a heat gun. ***Adult supervision is advised.*** Stop the flame with the wet cloth.

## PRO TIPS

· Using less water will give you a deeper color. Adding more water will make it more pastel-like.

· You can make these for outdoor use if you spray them heavily with silicone waterproofing spray.

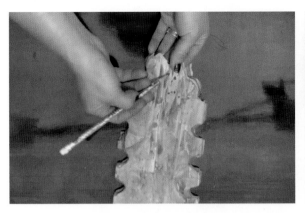

**14.** Straighten one end of an ornament hook, then poke a hole through the top of your assembled bags. Apply a ring of glue around the hole on both sides to prevent tearing the paper.

**15.** Glue the hook to the other side of the bags.

**16.** Stretch the bags open and loop your hook through the reinforced ring. Then hang and enjoy!

# Angel Faux Acrylic Painting

Painting with acrylic paint is something that many people enjoy. You can double-load your brush and do one-stroke painting to create beautiful flowers or implement tole painting to make adorable decorative images. One thing that distresses me about acrylic paint is that it's so heavily composed of plastics that the paintings always turn out with a high sheen. It also irritates me that I have to constantly wash out my brush. So, I have to dedicate time to do acrylic painting in order to save my brushes. It's also difficult to correct any mistakes. I am not really great at doing imagery artwork so a member of our SPiT FAMiLY, Regina (Kay) Richardson, is going to show you how she creates a beautiful angel that has so much depth and even a little texture.

## What you'll need

- **Unicorn SPiT colors:** White Ning, Zia, Lemon Kiss, Purple Hill Majesty, Blue Thunder, Weathered Daydream (used in wings), SQUiRREL (hair and flesh tone), Rustic Reality, and Pixie Punk Pink (limited use in flesh tone, wings, and gown)
- **Optional concept colors:** Stella (wings), Zeus (used in hair, halo, and very occasionally in the wings), Hephaestus (used in hair and halo), Selene (wings and gown), DiONYSUS (wings and background)

- **Optional SPARKLiNG SPiT:** Violet Vulture and Starling Sasha
- 18"x 24" canvas panel
- 1-inch angle brush (a flat brush will work just as well)
- Number 3 or number 5 round brush
- Water basin
- Blue shop towels
- Oil-based varnish/sealer
- Fine-mist spray bottle of water
- Palette paper, palette or paper plate(s)
- PiNCH Powder (optional for wing texture)

# Directions

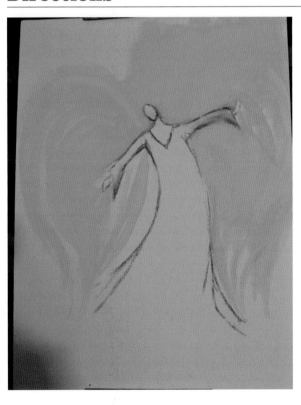

1. **Positioning:** Sketch in the basic figure on your canvas using charcoal or Blue Thunder thinned down with water, and your round brush. Both are very forgiving, so work with it until you get the basic placement. Proportion is not essential at this point, as this can be easily adjusted right up to sealing.

2. **Flow:** Use lines to create movement and feeling. A more vertical form with clasped hands and a bowed head might give a solemn or contemplative feeling. Drawing the face toward the sky and the palms upturned might give an entirely different feeling. This form could be carefree or even dancing.

3. **Wing Placement:** Use Lemon Kiss and a little White Ning to create placeholders for the wings and a glow behind the head and halo. Remember that neatness doesn't count but having fun does!

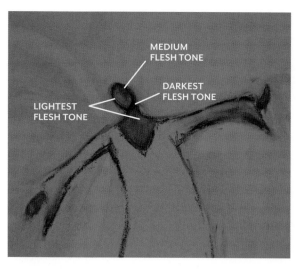

MEDIUM FLESH TONE

DARKEST FLESH TONE

LIGHTEST FLESH TONE

4. **Mixing Flesh Tones:** Add a BB-sized dot of SQUiRREL, Pixie Punk Pink, and Lemon Kiss to your palette. Add a pea-sized amount of White Ning. Barely touch your damp round brush into SQUiRREL, and then brush it off on a clean area of your palette. Pick up the tiniest bit of Lemon Kiss and mix it into the SQUiRREL, then repeat the process with the Pixie Punk Pink. The goal is to produce a mix resembling the darkest flesh tone in the photo.

5. Apply the darkest flesh tone to the shadow areas.

6. Use your dirty brush and dip it at least halfway into the White Ning. Remove and mix this in another clean area of your palette. Add White Ning until it reaches a middle tone of the complexion you want to achieve. Apply this to the rest of the face, neck, and hands.

7. Use your dirty brush to pick up more White Ning to mix the lightest flesh tone. Apply to the areas of the face, neck, and hands, as shown.

8. Remember, you are creating the impression of hands. Keep it simple; the viewer's eye will do the rest.

9. Shape the movement of the gown. Load your damp angle or flat brush with Blue Thunder. Using the chisel edge, begin with very little pressure at the shoulders and increase the pressure as you move down the garment. Mimic the curve you sketched in earlier. Add Zia for some lighter folds in the garment and Lemon Kiss for the very lightest. Use Purple Hill Majesty in the shadow areas and to narrow the chest area if needed.

10. **Shape the wings.** Load your angle or flat brush with Zia. Using the chisel edge, begin shaping the wings, picking up any of the colors of your palette. The goal is to make them mirror each other as much as possible. Notice that in the area inside the red box, I followed the flow of the gown and not the mirror of the other wing. I will correct that in the next step.

11. **Gaining perspective.** The head was too small in relation to the chest and arms, so as I lightened the face, I enlarged her head.

12. **Hair:** Using your clean, wet, round brush mix into the edge or your Purple Hill Majesty until it has the consistency of ink. Use this to paint the foundation of the hairstyle of your choice. You will add lighter strands in future steps, so solid coverage is not required.

**Note about correcting:** You will make strokes you do not like. Fortunately, Unicorn SPiT is very forgiving. Use a clean, damp, angle brush to redirect strokes or a clean, damp paper towel to remove what you don't like. These strokes are the initial layer and are to help you see the direction you would like the feathers to go so you can redirect these.

13. **Wing basecoat completion.** Use the angle brush to complete the basecoat for the wings using Blue Thunder, Zia, DiONYSUS, and White Ning, as desired.

14. **Second layer of hair.** Use the round brush in an inky mix of SQUiRREL and Lemon Kiss to add a few lighter strands of hair. After this layer is dry, add a little Zeus for some shimmer.

15. **Adding light to garment and wings.** Use the angle brush to add some White Ning or Selene to the wings and garment to lighten select areas. Then load some DiONYSUS or Atlantis and pull from the bottom of the garment toward the top to add some optional shimmer to the shadow areas of the gown. I turn the canvas upside down on the easel, because it is easier for me to pull down.

16. **Adding definition.** Use White Ning and Zia to continue defining the wings. In this step, I used very light pressure on the chisel edge of the angle brush to create these feather strokes. If you have Artemis and Selene, add those for some extra shimmer! If you like the wispy, ostrich plume type of feather, you can skip the additional wing steps.

17. If you want to incorporate some of the concept colors and metallics, take this opportunity to play. Use more pressure on the chisel edge to make quick strokes that will leave larger chunks of color. Use whatever colors you have on hand. You can also skip this step.

18. Use Selene and Artemis to continue lightening the garment. Deposit light/white in narrower areas right on top of the white that is already there.

19. Use the angle brush to add a mix of Lemon Kiss and White Ning above the head. Also, add Zeus and Selene to this area for a "glowing" effect.

20. Another optional step is to spray the dark areas at the bottom. Guard the wings with your other hand, unless you want the drippy effect to include the wing colors.

21. Use Hephaestus, Aphrodite, and Zeus (in that order) to add a final layer of light strands to the hair. You can use the SQUiRREL and Lemon Kiss mix with a small amount of White Ning to add lighter strands instead if you prefer. If you would like a blonde angel, you can add additional strands with a bit more white in the mix. If you accidentally go too light, use Rustic Reality to add your dark values back.

22. Use the round brush and Zeus to create the halo. Keep a clean, damp, angle or flat brush nearby in case you need to adjust. Add a very thin line of Hephaestus to the lower edges to give an illusion of roundness.

23. While you have Zeus on your round brush, add a little here and there to the sleeves, the dress, etc. I also added a bit of DiONYSUS here and there because I love it, and why not?

24. Mix an ounce of White Ning with PiNCH Powder to make a texture paste and let it set overnight. I used white so I could either leave it as white "feathers" or easily add another color to it or over it.

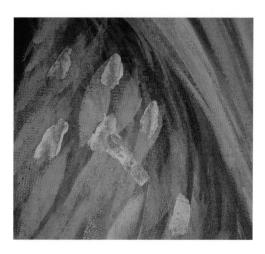

**25.** Use a small, pointed palette knife to get a small, marble-sized amount of the texture paste and place it on your palette. Use the knife to mix it to a smooth texture. I wanted the point of the feathers toward the bottom of the wing, so I turned the canvas upside down and pulled the texture paste of the palette knife.

**26.** Use Violet Vulture and Starling Sasha sparingly through the wings to add a pop of color and sparkle.

**27.** Use the angle brush and White Ning to reinforce the outside edges of the wings and the sleeve cuffs. Make sure there are no hard, dark lines remaining. They can distract from the other awesome strokes of color. Remember the sleeve on the right that had the hard purple line at the bottom?

**28.** I also noticed that I had overly lightened the face and neck. Nobody likes a pasty angel, not to mention that it made her very flat with no impression of roundness to the neck or face. Add some medium skin tone back into the shadow areas if this happens.

**29.** Use a varnish brush (or the softest brush you have) to apply two coats of oil-based topcoat. (**NOTE:** Varnish will intensify the colors, but not to the depth it appears in this photo.)

## PRO TIPS

- Step across the room from your painting and see what might need adjusting. Take a photo of your painting and see if anything looks off.
- Place less Unicorn SPiT on your palette than you think you'll need, especially if you are accustomed to using acrylics—it's the same effect.
- If you cannot complete all of the steps at once, walk away (and clean your brushes). Unicorn SPiT easily reactivates with a light mist of water!
- Always use high-quality paper towels when painting. Low-quality paper towels will disintegrate and leave a mess on your surface.
- You will make strokes you do not like. Unicorn SPiT is very forgiving.
- Use a clean, damp, angle brush to redirect strokes, or a clean, damp paper towel to remove what you do not like.

# Balloon Smash on Canvas

## What you'll need

- Unicorn SPiT colors: Purple Hill Majesty, Midnight's Blackness, and Blue Thunder
- White acrylic paint
- Three plastic cups
- Three wooden sticks
- Distilled water
- Inflated balloon
- Pouring medium
- Tacks
- Paint strainer
- Non-yellowing oil spray

Modern abstract art has become so popular because of its beautiful, airy, organic look, as well as the mesmerizing flow of colors. One of my SPiT FAMiLY members, Stephanie Keene, is here to show you how she uses Unicorn SPiT in her flow arts using a balloon to create these beautiful blooming flowers.

# Directions

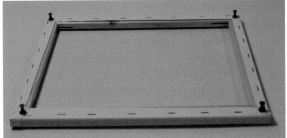

1. Place tacks on the underside of the board to elevate the surface. I like to use a Gesso board.

2. Filter the pouring medium/paint extender through a paint strainer to remove any solid bits.

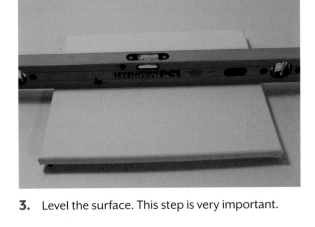

3. Level the surface. This step is very important.

4. Mix 1 oz. of Purple Hill Majesty with 4 oz. of pouring medium/paint extender.

5. Mix 1 oz. of Blue Thunder and 4 tsp. of Midnight's Blackness with 4 oz. of pouring medium.

6. Mix 4 oz. of white acrylic paint with 4 oz. of pouring medium and 1 oz. of distilled water.

7. Spread the white paint across the board, tilting the board back and forth to cover the entire surface. It is important to allow the paint to self-level.

## PRO TIP

· When working on a canvas, it's helpful to place a box underneath to firm up the surface.

**8.** Pool the purple and blue paint in puddles across the board.

**9.** Press an inflated balloon into the paint until your design is achieved. Be careful not to overwork the paint.

**10.** Allow 24 to 48 hours for the paint to dry.

**11.** Wait five days for the paint to cure before sealing.

# CHAPTER SEVEN

# Clay, Concrete, and Plaster

There's no reason you can't add color to hard, porous, surfaces, including concrete floors. Because Unicorn SPiT is so concentrated, you're never going to be limited financially with how big or little you can blaze your colors. Not everyone thinks about adding color to a flowerpot or a plain concrete floor. Plaster and clay and concrete artists will delight with the way that Unicorn SPiT can bring nontoxic color to garden art, porcelain, paper clay sculptures, and even your concrete floor. There is virtually no porous surface that Unicorn SPiT can't bless with whichever magnificent colors flow from your imagination.

# Paper Clay

## What you'll need

- Unicorn SPiT: SQUiRREL, Lemon Kiss, Midnight's Blackness, and Dragon's Belly
- Concept color: Selene
- White texture paint
- 8"x 8" canvas
- Décor Molds called Forest Treasures by Re-design by Prima
- Corn starch
- Spray varnish
- E6000

Paper clay and stone clay work about the same and are very fragile. They're prone to chips and breaks and cracks. Cindi Deniece Carpenter has taken her clay art to a whole new level by staining it with Unicorn SPiT as opposed to painting. If her work were to get chipped or scratched, the white of the clay itself wouldn't be revealed because Unicorn SPiT pigmentation absorbs deep into the surface. Now you can create your wildest desires without the worry of lasting durability.

# Directions

1. Cover the canvas with acrylic white texture paint.

2. Load your brush with SQUiRREL and dab off. Lightly drag your brush across the canvas allowing the color to hit the highest parts of the texture.

3. Cover the canvas with a piece of rubber shelf liner. Lightly pad the liner down to get a textured appearance.

4. Lightly dust the mold with cornstarch so that the stone clay doesn't stick.

## PRO TIPS

- The details on the flowers from the Re-design Décor Molds are so amazing and using Unicorn SPiT made it so easy to blend my colors.
- The great part is if you don't like it, just rinse it off and start over.

5. Push stone clay into the mold using your thumb. You can use a plastic card, such as a credit card, to smooth it down and get rid of excess clay. Let it sit for a few minutes, then unmold it.

6. Repeat the process to get all of the mold pieces you need. Let them dry flat and SPiT all pieces with a base coat of Selene.

7. Use Lemon Kiss, SQUiRREL, and Midnight's Blackness to blend the petals and the single flower. Use SQUiRREL, Midnight's Blackness, and Selene for the middle of the Sunflower. Add Dragon's Belly with a little Midnight's Blackness for the leaves.

8. After they're dry, seal with oil-based or spray clear sealent.

9. Arrange the pieces onto the canvas and before gluing them down, take a small paintbrush mixed with SQUiRREL and Midnight's Blackness. Paint a shadow effect under the flower pieces. I used E6000 to glue them down.

# Cactus Pot

Houseplants bring such beauty to your home. They generate fresh air and it's wonderful to have something to care for—they are like a stationary pet. We get our doggies and kitties fun collars, why not do it for our flora friends? You can easily color and create a cute outfit for any one of your plants to complement them or the room's decor. Garage sales and estate sales are my absolute favorite place to find clay pots. The longer you have your plants, the more often you'll have to put them in bigger pots. There's no need to buy expensive pots when you can design your own. Find one that will give your plant room to grow. Get a designer look at a fraction of the price.

## What you'll need

- Unicorn SPiT colors: Phoenix Fire, Blue Thunder, Zia, and Midnight's Blackness
- Clean terracotta pot
- Jumbo flat brush
- Wide-tip brush
- Medium round brush
- Hair dryer
- Spray bottle of water
- Lazy Susan
- Silicone waterproofing spray or matte-finish topcoat

147

# Directions

1. Put your pot centered on a Lazy Susan. Dip your brush into Phoenix Fire and place it on the surface of the pot. Turn the Lazy Susan to create a solid band around the pot. Make three bands.

2. Dip your brush in Blue Thunder and spin your way to creating three more bands, leaving room for one more color.

3. Dip your brush in the Zia and spin again to create more bands where you see fit. Don't be afraid to overlap on the blue because it looks pretty. Overlapping on the orange, not so much.

4. We are going to triple-load our jumbo artist's brush by dipping it into all three colors at one time. Just put a dab of each color next to one other on a palette.

5. Take your triple-loaded brush, touch it to the brim of your pot, and give it a spin. You're going to love how these colors blend in such a crazy way.

**6.** Load your brush with Zia and paint the rim and inside of the brim.

**7.** If you want to blend more, spray your wide-tip brush with water.

**8.** Put the wet, clean brush on your freshly painted bands on the pot and give it a spin to make the colors all blend. Be sure to clean your brush before moving to a new area if your brush isn't big enough to cover the whole surface from top to bottom.

**9.** Let it dry naturally or blow-dry.

**10.** Dip your brush in Midnight's Blackness and spin yourself a nice black band at the base of your pot.

**11.** Make a pile of Midnight's Blackness and mist it with water to create a more liquid consistency. Do not completely dissolve the color.

**12.** Touch your medium round brush to the bottom of the Zia band, pulling down into the black band at the bottom. Then reload your brush, move it over a few inches, and touch your pot on the upper orange band with a downward stroke to the bottom. This creates long and short cactus centers. Continue this long-short, long-short pattern along the pot.

**13.** Just off to the side of each cactus center, touch your brush to the pot, pull downward just a bit, and pull inward back toward the center. Do this on both sides of each cactus for both the long and the short ones. Feel free to touch your brush to the base of each cactus on its side, creating the look of rocks or prickly pear cacti. Don't worry about your brush strokes. They'll disappear upon sealing.

**14.** Let it dry. Spray with silicone waterproofing spray or matte finish topcoat to maintain the chalky look of pottery.

## PRO TIPS

- Sealing the exterior is not necessarily going to make it extremely water-resistant. To achieve that, you will need to thoroughly coat the interior of the pot with waterproofing spray for semi-waterproofing, or epoxy for a super-waterproof seal. As is, it's perfectly durable for low-moisture plants like succulents and cacti.
- To create a fire-glazed look, cover the exterior and interior with epoxy.
- Creating silhouettes is one of the easiest and most recognizable objects that you can paint.

# Ceramic Diffuser

Aromatherapy is something that I truly believe in. I have seen the benefits while working with the elderly and disabled and while calming my children when they were babies. It also helps me immerse myself in a creative environment. Diffusers are readily available everywhere, from the local grocery store to dollar stores. It's wonderful to be able to pour in a mood-inducing scent, put it on a shelf, and allow the scent to travel up the wick and cast its magic throughout the room. But did you know that aromatherapy oils can lock the color of Unicorn SPiT into its diffusing catalyst? Now there's no reason that you can't add color and turn these plain white clay diffusers into little works of art.

## What you'll need

- Unicorn SPiT color: Pixie Punk Pink
- SPARLiNG Unicorn SPiT color: Golden Gosling
- New wicking ceramic flower diffuser
- Small round artist brush
- Fine-tip artist brush
- Spray bottle of water

# Directions

1. Remove the top of the diffuser and separate it from the base. Tie the wick in a knot to keep it out of the way and to make it easier to handle. If you can remove the flower, then go for it. If not, it's okay. Mine was glued on.

2. Add some water to the center of your paint palette. Add a drop of Pixie Punk Pink in a separate area of your palette. Dip your brush into the pink, then into the water, then swirl your brush around to create the perfect tone of watery pink. You can add more Pixie Punk Pink to the water, but I've found that a little pink goes a long way. This watery dye will easily absorb into the pores of the diffuser flower.

3. When you pick up your brush from the pink dye, allow the excess to drip off. Then gradually color each petal, beginning with the ends of the petal. Work your way in toward the base. The color will absorb rapidly so you will need to reload your brush often. You can do an additional coat of color toward the ends of each petal to add more interest.

## PRO TIP

- You can speckle your flower by randomly tapping your brush with the colors of your choice and letting the dye droplets stand and absorb slowly.

**4.** Put a little Golden Gosling on your palette. You won't need much, but you'll be using it at full strength.

**5.** Dip your smaller brush into the Golden Gosling and apply to the deepest part of each petal toward the middle, pulling outward and over the pink just a bit.

**6.** Not going all the way to the edge with the Golden Gosling and keeping it in the center will give it a pretty glow. Allow it to dry for 24 hours. There is no need to seal this, as the aromatherapy oil you choose will seal the diffuser as it flows up the wick and into the flower.

## PRO TIPS

· After the diffuser is dry and before it's infused with oil, you can add more color if you'd like.

· You can use this process on any clay or stone diffuser that hasn't been exposed to oil.

# Exterior Plaster Wall Art

I love working in my garden. I feel like my garden is an extension of my home, but instead of couches and tables, I have rose bushes and hostas. So it makes sense that I like to hang garden art on my fence or exterior walls just as I would in my family room.

Terri Viner-Billett enjoys pouring plaster and cement (check) into molds to create beautiful garden art and color them with rich, earthy colors—and sometimes bright ones—to bring her artwork into the garden along with her green thumb.

## What you'll need

- Latex molds with or without a support case, or a solid mold
- Choose your medium: cement, plaster, or stone cast plaster that is weatherproof
- Rubber bucket or large bowl
- Large wooden spoon
- For larger amounts of mixture, use a professional plasterer's mixing tool you can attach to an electric drill
- Plastic sheeting
- Spray bottle of water with a tiny amount of dish soap
- Level surface with a large box or container filled with damp sand
- Rubber gloves
- Blunt knitting needles
- Skewers or chopsticks
- Spatula
- Shop towel
- Dust mask
- Hook or whatever you plan to use to hang your item on the wall

## Directions

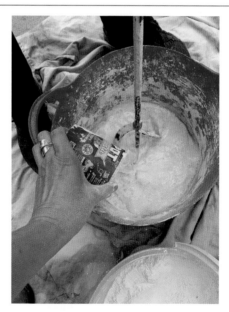

1. Place your chosen mold into the damp sand, making sure it is level and not distorted. Use the sand to support the mold by either mounding it around the mold or by digging out a space in the sand and then gently filling around it. Even if you are using a solid mold or a support case, you will still need to prop it up in the sandbox to ensure it is level.

2. Spray your mold with the water and dishwashing liquid mix—just a little though. This will help your medium flow into all the details of your mold and minimize bubbles.

3. Mix your medium as per the instructions. It should be a thick, creamy consistency, but loose enough to pour. Bang your bucket a few times to help air bubbles rise and pop.

4. Slowly pour into your molds and use your skewer/chopstick to gently ease it into all the details of your mold. When it's full, you can use your spatula to level out the top if needed and to break any bubbles that rise.

5. Let it partly dry and then place a hook or hanger of choice on the back. You can also sign your work at this stage using your skewer.

6. Let it completely dry, then demold the items made with stonecast within two hours. Be careful, as they will be warm and can damage easily at this stage. It's not recommended to leave items made with stonecast plaster in the mold for longer than two hours as they need airflow to properly set.

## PRO TIPS

- I find that pushing Rawl plugs partway through the setting stage makes it easy to put screws in and use a strong wire to hang up your piece after the piece dries.
- You can use solid plastic molds, but these are only plaque-type molds. There are many options to choose from.
- Be aware that latex molds with support cases are more costly.
- Plaster of paris will dry quickly and you'll be able to demold within two to four hours. Set your piece aside overnight before painting it.
- Concrete is less likely to dry fast. I normally leave these items overnight before attempting to demold.
- Wash your molds and equipment thoroughly after each use, seal all powder bags, and keep them in a dry place.
- Mixing guides are normally on the packet, but as a rule of thumb, if you are using concrete it's 1 part concrete to 2 parts sharp sand mix.

# Now, here's the fun part. It's time to start SPiTTiNG!

## Directions

1. Decide which color tones you want by mixing them. There are so many colors in the range that often I don't need to mix.

2. Lay your object on plastic or an old cloth. Cloth is better because it will absorb drips and your hands won't get covered in paint.

3. The first thing to do is to seal the object. It doesn't matter what you've used to cast it, it's going to be absorbent and will suck up your Unicorn SPiT—although less so if you've used stone cast, which dries to a smooth firm finish. Give it a quick spray of matte semi-gloss sealer.

4. Once that's dry, you can begin to paint. If you want to go for a Verdigris finish, paint the item with a green-blue shade. Allow that to dry, then spray with matte sealer.

5. Go over the top with your chosen metallic shade, then wipe it back to reveal the green in all the fine detail of the item. You can do this the other way around, too, starting with the metallic paint and then the green-blue.

6. If you want your items to be painted in detail, the same rules apply: Seal each layer with the matte spray—it stops color bleed and avoids wiping off what you've already painted. Because Unicorn SPiT is water-based, if it's glazed between layers, any mistake can be wiped away easily without ruining the work you've already done.

7. Use your Unicorn SPiT the same way you would watercolors. The effects are very similar. And always allow plenty of drying time before you spray your seal. Remember to paint the back of your item and glaze it. If it's going outside, you will want it to be completely waterproof.

8. When you're happy with how the Unicorn SPiT looks, finish your piece by giving it a spray of gloss or semi-gloss sealer. This really deepens the colors and produces an almost kiln-fired glazed finish. But you can finish with a matte sealer if you prefer. You have so many painting options, whether it's highly detailed or a simple finish.

# Vibrant Concrete Floor

Carpet, tile, and vinyl flooring can drain a design budget. If you want some fancy, artistic-looking designs, you're going to pay through the teeth. If you have a concrete floor, why not just utilize it as a canvas and replicate or create your own beautiful design. This can save you a considerable amount of money. People's astonishment when you tell them you did it is priceless. It's a rarity for someone to compliment your room and comment about your carpet, but it won't be a rarity when they compliment your art. You will be surprised how simple and economical this is.

## What you'll need

- Unicorn SPiT colors: your choice
- Concept color metallics: your choice
- Smooth, level concrete floor
- Vacuum
- Flooring epoxy
- 1-inch and 3-inch paint flat brushes
- Large buckets or containers for each color

# Directions

1. If your concrete floor is free of glues and rough edges, and it's nice and smooth, then you are ready to start. Just pop off the baseboards if you can. My floors were a mess. One side was covered in glue from cheap carpet, while the other was covered in tile adhesive, grout, and tile. I hired a guy to remove the tile, glue, and baseboards. He made the floor smooth by using a concrete floor grinder.

2. If you need to grind your floor, vacuum up as much of the dust and debris as you can. I also swept and vacuumed all the walls and the ceiling, creating as much of a dust-free room as I could to make sure nothing would drop off when it came time to seal.

3. Use a piece of sidewalk chalk to draw your design onto the concrete. Then mix 1 part Unicorn SPiT with 10 parts water.

4. Using your brushes, color in your design using this watery, concrete stain mixture. Some colors may take two coats. I noticed that I had to do two coats with Zia. In hindsight, I could have diluted with 5 parts water.

**6.** After your base colors are dry, feel free to come back and highlight using your favorite METALLiCS.

**5.** Be sure to start in the back and work your way out, leaving the part near the exit for last. Do not walk on your colors while they're wet. They dry quickly so you should be able to walk on them in your socks or bare feet within a few hours.

**7.** Allow your design to dry for 24 to 48 hours, depending on humidity. You will know it's ready to seal when the entire floor looks extremely matte and chalky. When you're sure the floor is dry, seal it with your favorite flooring epoxy or 3–4 coats of oil-based concrete sealer. Once your topcoat is cured, put your baseboards back on and enjoy your new floor.

NOTE: It took 84 oz. of Unicorn SPiT to cover 800 sq. ft. of concrete when using 1 part Unicorn SPiT to 10 parts water. When I was finished, there was a little of each color left, so before I sealed the floor, I added a second coat of color to the parts I wanted to make more vibrant.

## PRO TIPS

- If you're unable to bend over for long periods of time to SPiT, tape your paintbrush to a broomstick. Use electrical tape because painter's tape is not strong enough to hold the brush.
- You can do any of the stain-press techniques on concrete floors as well. Just buy the largest clear drop cloths you can. That way, you're able to color large areas at a time.
- You can color exterior concrete as well. Just be sure to use an oil-based concrete sealant that has UV protection.

# Alcohol iNK Coasters

## What you'll need

- Unicorn SPiT colors: Phoenix Fire, Molly Red Pepper, Pixie Punk Pink, and Purple Hill Majesty
- Respirator
- Embossing gun or hair dryer
- Ceramic tile (quantity, size, and shape of your choice)
- Small mixing containers
- 71 percent isopropyl alcohol
- Aerosol varnish, spray clear engine enamel, or epoxy resin such as FAMOWOOD Glaze Coat
- Cork for the bottom
- Plastic sheeting to protect your work surface

I like to go on YouTube for inspiration to find out about new mediums I haven't tried before. What caught my attention recently was alcohol inks. I love the way they looked—like watercolor but it could go on so many surfaces including glass and photo paper and, in this case, tile. It seems like a really fun process because there are different heating tools and even fire to get different effects. It seemed like an artist's adventure to me, so I knew I had to try it.

I decided to try to make my own alcohol ink as opposed to investing hundreds of dollars into a new art medium. Low and behold, after some trial and error, I was able to figure it out. I'm excited to say that this DiY Alcohol iNK recipe is a great success and Kim Cook, who is well experienced using alcohol ink, is here to show you how she uses the Unicorn SPiT recipe to make beautiful tile alcohol ink coasters.

# Directions

1. There are two methods of adding alcohol to SPiT: you can premix in containers to your desired saturation, or you can place a small amount of SPiT onto your tile and drop the alcohol right on top. Practice a bit to feel how the SPiT moves in the alcohol as well as how it moves on different surfaces.

2. Once the SPiT and alcohol are mixed, drop the DiY Alcohol iNK with a dropper, or carefully pour it onto the tile.

3. Immediately push it back and forth with your embossing gun or hair dryer.

4. From this point, colors can be added the same way, one on top of the other.

5. This would be a good time to stop or even add a little embellishment. Place a stencil on the tile at the corner and then using a cloth with alcohol on it, wipe back the dry mixture.

## PRO TIPS

- When working with alcohol, there is one important point to consider—safety. Alcohol is toxic and affects some more than others. Although you may not smell it, it is there and being inhaled, so the use of a respirator is necessary. The preferred type is one that filters fumes and vapors.

- When creating art with DiY Alcohol iNK, the better surfaces are the slick ones, as they do not allow any penetration into the surface. The most popular is Yupo Paper. Yupo is a synthetic paper made from polypropylene pellets. Imagine it as plastic paper. It is super-smooth, durable, won't tear, holds the alcohol well, and cleans up well if you make a mistake.

- Other types of paper you can use are glossy photo paper and watercolor paper, which must first be "primed" with a gel medium. Once the gel dries it will be waterproof.

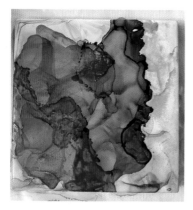

**6.** Layer Zia, Pixie Punk Pink, Molly Red Pepper, and Purple Hill Majesty, one color at a time.

**7.** The next step is fun as well as cathartic. Fill a small container with alcohol and select a small artist's brush. Dip the brush into the alcohol and then begin dotting the dry tile. Keep going until it looks complete.

**8.** Once everything is dry, it's time to seal. Start with two to three coats of matte aerosol varnish made for protecting acrylic or water-color paintings, then follow up with either clear engine enamel or resin. The bottoms can be lined with cork or rubber bumpers. For this project, the coasters were coated with heat-resistant resin for the final seal coat.

## PRO TIPS

- Because Unicorn SPiT is water-based, use an oil-based sealer. Alcohol can also reactivate with oil-based sealers, so it is recommended to begin with two to three coats of matte aerosol varnish made for protecting acrylic or watercolor paintings. It will not activate the alcohol, it will prevent any yellowing, and it will seal the color.

- After the piece has been sealed, layer with additional types of sealer, depending on the end-use of the project. For coasters, use a heat-resistant epoxy/resin to prevent hot mugs from sticking to the coaster. Another option for coasters is spray Engine Enamel, which is oil-based and heat-resistant. If you have completed your project on primed wood, then any oil-based sealer would be appropriate.

# CHAPTER EIGHT

# Plastic and Cast Resin

Plastics are a magnificent invention. From cleaning bottles to laminate countertops, you can walk into a thrift store and find an abundance of hard plastic decor to choose from. You can even upcycle disposable plastic and cast resin containers into reusable, artistic, eco-friendly works of art. Unicorn SPiT is a lot of fun to use on plastics because if you don't like what you did, you can easily wash it off and play with the idea again and again.

# Cosplay Shield

### What you'll need

- Unicorn SPiT SPARKLiNG: a variety of colors
- Concept color: Zeus
- 2 mm EVA (Ethylene-Vinyl Acetate) foam
- 4 or 6 mm EVA foam
- Worbla TranspArt
- Decoupage
- Polyurethane - floor wax
- Exacto knife
- Contact cement
- Superglue
- Acrylic paints for base layer on EVA foam
- Exacto knife

Avera Cosplay is deep into cosplay—performance art where individuals dress up in costume to represent a certain character. Video games and comic books can entertain you, but how much fun would it be to create your own costume and become one of the characters yourself? That's exactly what Avera Cosplay does and the costume designs and props that she makes look like they come right off a Hollywood set. She has even won awards at various comic conventions. In this project, she's going to show you how she creates her beautiful Worbla shield.

# Directions

1. Find or create your pattern. There are two options: Find an image that is already stained glass or find a simple design you can alter to create the stained-glass appearance. Coloring-book pages are a good source for simple images and designs that can easily be turned into stained glass. Just make sure that your lines are relatively thick. If the foam is very thin, the Unicorn SPiT could bleed. Also, it is not as sturdy. Cut out the parts of the pattern that will be the glass, using the Exacto knife.

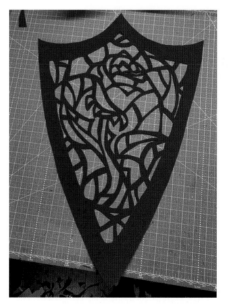

2. The foam will act as your pattern and to give structure to the Worbla. Transfer the pattern to both 2-mm and 4-mm EVA foam, and using the Exacto knife, cut out the pattern. The 2 mm will be the front of the glass and the thicker foam will be the back. Heat-seal the foam by using a heat gun.

**3.** Transparent Worbla usually comes in rolls, so you will need to heat it up to get all the wrinkles out. Transparent Worbla will stick to itself, so make sure it does not touch itself when heated. Trace the base shape of the object and cut it out with scissors.

**4.** Apply a generous layer of decoupage to the Worbla. You do not have to let it dry. Place the 2 mm top layer on the top of the Worbla and add more decoupage. This will glue the top layer to the Worbla but it will dry clear. In addition, it helps to absorb the Unicorn SPiT and seals the 2 mm foam for painting. Let this layer dry. If there are gaps between the foam and the Worbla that both heat and decoupage are not resolving, you can use super glue to make sure the foam and Worbla are connected. If there is a gap, the colors will bleed into each other.

5. I've used the Unicorn SPiT SPARKLiNG version here, which is thinner and more transparent than the standard SPiT formulas. Decoupage will keep the SPiT stuck to the Worbla and it also helps the SPiT dry translucent. Mix Unicorn SPiT SPARKLiNG to decoupage in a 70/30 ratio. That will help to increase opacity and speed up the drying time. If you use other formulas of Unicorn SPiT, you will have to mix with more decoupage at least 50/50 to get the translucent effect. Do not apply it thicker than the foam or it will spill over.

6. Let it dry. It's going to take a while, depending on how thick it was applied. Do not touch it or fix it. Let it do its thing. It may appear to be pulling away from the edge or you may see bubbles, but that's okay. Glass is not perfect. It may look as if it's losing its color, but it's not. Once it's sealed, it will be vibrant again.

NOTE: Right now, the stain is attached to the decoupage for the most part. If you mess with it, it will peel. It may take up to 48 hours to dry completely. If you must add a dab or two to any mistakes or areas you are not happy with, that's okay, so long as it's dried.

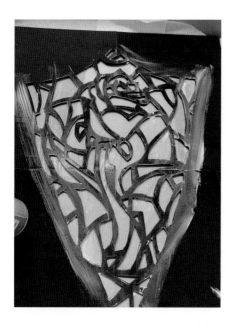

7. Assemble the back. Using the thicker foam, follow the same steps as the 2 mm. Treat it with the heat gun and then seal it with decoupage. You will want to put small dots of super-glue around each part of the design to attach the foam to the back side of the Worbla.

## PRO TIPS

- You can mix colors directly into the cell to add depth and shading.
- You can also mix colors and decoupage first, and then apply them.
- I use squeeze bottles to apply, squeezing the SPiT in a circular motion.
- You can also play with the ratios of decoupage to get different levels of opacity.

8. **Optional:** I added more details to the shield, but this is not necessarily specific to the stained-glass effect and may or may not be relevant to your project. I added another border to the 4-mm foam back using contact cement. I drew a wood-grain pattern and wood-burned the pattern into the foam. I made the strap from 2-mm foam and the handle from 4-mm foam. The rivets on the front and back are painted googly eyes. I created foam flowers and filigrees by pressing foam clay into silicone cake molds. I put the molds in the freezer for 15 minutes to help them form quickly and dry faster. All these details were sealed with decoupage.

9. If you are using black acrylic paint, you will want to go over the black foam on the stained glass. This will clean it up a bit if there was any SPiT that spilled over.

10. Seal with an oil-based sealer. Polyurethane will give it a gloss that helps the glass effect. Sealing it will bring the colors back to life as well as protect the shield from peeling or cracking. You can also use epoxy or lacquer on the SPiT, depending on the project and how flexible you need it to be.

## PRO TIP

- Use black foam to minimize painting. I used a gliding wax for the base layer of gold, then I used concept color Zeus to help the details pop.

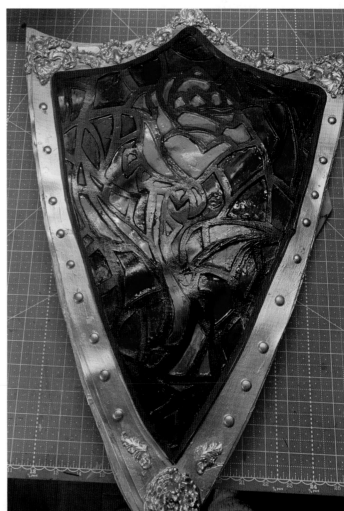

# Faux Tarnished Brass Mirror Frame

My local discount store had some tacky gold picture frames. They looked super cheap, but I knew that the detail they had would look absolutely beautiful if I SPiT them and accentuated the design. I decided that this frame needed to look like it was old and tarnished by time. Let me show you how I transformed this cheap plastic picture frame into a Victorian-style tabletop mirror by doing a quick antiquing technique. Don't feel limited to do this on plastic. You can do this on any sealed item that you want to give an antiqued look. This project was so easy to do that it really is instant gratification.

## What you'll need

- Unicorn SPiT color: Midnight's Blackness
- Plastic or resin metallic-finished frame or mirror with architectural interest
- Medium chalk paintbrush
- Spray bottle of water
- Shop cloth
- Hair dryer to speed up the drying process

# Directions

1. Begin by removing the back of the frame as well as the glass or tape as best you can to protect it. Apply a bead of Midnight's Blackness onto the entire frame.

2. Use your brush to move the color around, covering the entire surface, especially all of the little grooves, gaps, and sides.

3. Let it dry. You'll know that it's dry when it becomes chalky looking.

4. Wrap the shop cloth around your finger and mist water.

5. Use the damp cloth to lightly buff the raised areas of the frame, exposing the gold on the tips and leaving the Midnight's Blackness in the lower areas, crevices, and grooves.

## PRO TIPS

- You can turn any picture frame into a mirror with mirror spray paint.
- If you feel that you've removed too much Midnight's Blackness, you can always add more and repeat the process.
- If brass isn't your style, you can do faux tarnish on silver, copper, or even wood tones. This antiquing style can be used on anything you want to give this tarnished, glaze look.

6. Allow your piece to dry, reassemble it, and it's ready to use. If desired, seal with an oil-based topcoat in your preferred finish. I do not recommend wax to seal plastics.

# Faux Patina Candlestick

Creating a collection from mismatched, random decorative accessories is super easy and inexpensive. Keep an open mind when you're shopping. Don't look at the color, just think of the shape. As you can see in this collection, I took a cheap picture frame, a random candlestick, and a wooden frame and made them all match with this simple bright and cheery patina technique.

## What you'll need

- Unicorn SPiT colors: Blue Thunder Navajo Jewel, and Zia
- Plastic or resin, elaborate candlestick
- Spray bottle of water
- Shop cloth
- Medium chalk paintbrush
- Palette

# Directions

1. Prepare your candlestick by painting it your favorite metallic color. I chose gold.

2. Triple-load your large brush by making separate puddles of Blue Thunder and Navajo Jewel. Put Zia in the middle. Make your chain of colors as wide as your brush so when you dip it, you will get all three colors at one time.

3. Apply the colors thickly onto the candlestick, allowing the paint to fall into every crevice. You can do this all the way around, including the top. Let it dry.

4. Use the damp cloth to lightly buff the raised areas of the candlestick, revealing as little of the base tone as you like and leaving the colors within the deep nooks and crannies. You can remove as much or as little as you like.

5. You can use a dry area of your cloth to buff any color residue and make it shiny again.

## PRO TIPS

- You can do this technique on any surface, including sealed and finished furniture.
- There is no need to seal if you are fine with dry dusting and if you would like to change the color scheme later on. All you need to do is wash it off with a little water.

# Colorizing Doll Hair

## What you'll need

- Two to three tones of Unicorn SPiT
- A doll with synthetic, light-colored hair
- Toothbrush
- Fine-tooth stylist comb
- Medium-size artist brush
- Hair dryer
- Palette

I remember as a little girl enjoying endless hours playing with my dolls. I can only imagine how much more fun I would have had if I could pretend I was a colorful hairstylist at a salon and my dolls were my clients. Heck, I liked doing this as an adult! It's so much fun picking out thrift store dolls, bringing them home, and giving them a whole new life. Remember, as always, that adult supervision is recommended, which makes this a great opportunity to bond with your little ones while doing this project together.

# Directions

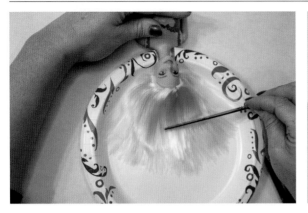

1. Place your doll down, allowing her hair to flow onto a disposable plate. Use your comb to fan the doll's hair out.

2. Put your colors of choice on your palette. Wet your brush with water, dip into your SPiT, and apply stripes of color from the root of the doll's head to the ends.

3. Another way to apply color is to double-load a toothbrush with two colors you like.

4. Then you can simply brush the color into your doll's hair.

5. Dry your doll's hair on low or no heat until dry. You can easily comb and blow dry as you go.

6. Once dried and combed, your doll's hair will be tinted a beautiful color for you to play with or style.

**7.** When you're ready to change your doll's hair color, you can wash it out easily with shampoo. Let it dry and color again.

**8.** Have fun experimenting with all of your favorite colors.

## PRO TIPS

- Applying petroleum jelly to the doll's forehead, neck, shoulders, and anywhere you don't want the colors to reach, is a great way to protect those areas from getting stained.

- If the color does not want to completely wash out, rinse with a bit of bleach water and shampoo until all residual color is gone.

# Marbled Spray Bottle

Lots of manufacturers are putting cleaning agents in disposable spray bottles that have super-awesome pumps that spray out a mist fancy-like. It's a shame to throw them away. When I saw how nice these were, the first thing I thought of was how wonderful they would be to use to water my orchids. Instead of digging out the bottles from under the sink, I decided to make one beautiful enough to leave out and complement my little window orchid garden. Even my kids feel the desire to water my babies for me because I guess the bottle looks that enchanting.

## What you'll need

- Unicorn SPiT colors: Navajo Jewel and White Ning
- Cuptisserie
- Epoxy, like FAMOWOOD Glaze Coat
- Re·Design with Prima Decor Transfer
- Plastic wrap
- Hair dryer
- Electrical tape
- Alcohol
- Popsicle sticks
- Torch
- Plastic spray bottle

# Directions

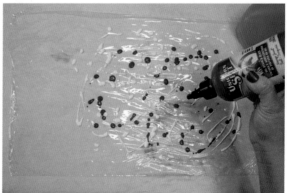

1. Use a sufficient amount of popsicle sticks wide enough to snugly sit inside the opening of the bottle. This will become your handle that will also fit into your cuptisserie bracket.

2. Use electrical tape to secure the popsicle sticks to the bottle. Make sure you wrap the tape around the areas where the spray head would connect to protect it. Add more popsicle sticks to the end of the handle to be sure it will fit snugly inside the cuptisserie bracket.

3. Cut a piece of plastic wrap that's large enough to wrap around the bottle. Drizzle Navajo Jewel and White Ning here and there on the plastic wrap, concentrating mostly on the center. It's always good to use more white to achieve multitones of whatever color you decide to put with it.

4. Lay the side of your bottle in the middle of your colorful concoction.

## PRO TIP

· Make sure the popsicle stick handle you make fits snug enough that it will not come loose from your cuptisserie bracket.

5. Grab the ends of the plastic wrap. Lift up and bring them together at the middle of the bottle, allowing the colorful mixture to wrap around the back of the bottle.

6. Using your hands, smoosh the colors around under the plastic wrap, stretching the color to cover the bottle entirely, including the bottom.

**7.** Remove plastic wrap to reveal a beautiful, marbled look.

**8.** Let it dry (**warning**: using a hair drying on a high setting may cause cracking).

**9.** Lay the bottle down on a non-abrasive surface. Select a Re·Design with Prima Decor Transfer and decide its placement. Lay the transfer directly onto the dried Unicorn SPiT, then gently rub the transfer with a popsicle stick.

**10.** Starting with one end of your transfer, rub with the popsicle stick as you pull the transfer sheet to reveal the image on your bottle.

**11.** Attach the handle to the cuptisserie bracket. Turn on the machine and coat your bottle with epoxy.

**12.** Wisp the epoxy with a flame to pop the bubbles. Be careful not to overheat because the plastic will melt easily.

**13.** Use alcohol to wipe away any excess epoxy that may inhibit the spray head from reconnecting.

**14.** Allow to spin and cure for at least 12 hours or follow the manufacturer's curing time. After the epoxy is set up and cured, remove the handle, reassemble, and mist your little heart out.

## PRO TIPS

- You can add a little glitter to your epoxy for a really glam look. If you're like me and like the look but not the mess of glitter, you can add it directly into the epoxy when mixing and the glitter will be encapsulated and suspended. It won't come off and leave glitter trails anywhere you use it.

- If you want to paint the spray head and handle, make sure to put a piece of painter's tape on the hole in the nozzle where the water comes out.

- You can use this process on flowerpots to match your water bottle or easily redesign any containers to match your decor.

# CHAPTER NINE

# Fluid Arts

There's something magical that occurs and makes you feel like an artistic chemist when you play with fluid arts. Fluid art is taking colorful liquid art medium and pouring it onto any substrate using it as a canvas to create a mesmerizing kaleidoscope of intricate details. The guesswork, the anticipation, the thrill, and the outcome are a surprise and unique every single time. Never will you get the same outcome twice, even if you use the same colors and process. This art requires letting go of expectations and riding it like a roller coaster. It will excite your senses with the vivid colors and the natural flow of liquids that you're able to capture.

This is becoming my favorite art practice for when I'm down to the last bit of SPiT in the bottle. I'll add my water and pouring medium and shake up my bottles getting every last drop of pigment. Then I'll save it for when it's time to unleash my inner fluid beast. One thing you will find is that Unicorn SPiT is more powerful than any paint on the market. It is the most economical and vibrant pigment to use in fluid arts that you can find.

# Faux Amethyst Bowl

## What you'll need

- Unicorn SPiT DiY Alcohol iNK colors in pink, blue, and gold (see page 13)
- Broken colored tempered glass or glass glitter
- Plastic wrapped Lazy Susan with a lip (this will keep the epoxy from spilling over)
- Pint of epoxy, like FAMOWOOD Glaze Coat
- Plastic-wrapped tall vase or bowl
- Rubber gloves
- Level work surface

Natural minerals such as crystals and geodes mesmerize me. They fascinate a lot of people, as seen by the variety of mineral shows that take place. As you may know, these mineral formations can go for a pretty penny. I would love to have a giant amethyst geode that I could stand in. But for now, I will have to settle for small geodes used for paperweights and bookends and create my own free-form sculptures that resemble these high-ticket items.

I happened to have a bunch of broken tempered glass that a friend gave me. I thought it was really pretty and it reminded me of crystals. I experimented a time or two, pouring tinted epoxy over the glass to create jewel-encrusted effects in some laser-cut signs and formed a shape of the cross on a board. But this time, I was feeling adventurous. I wanted to try a new way to tint the epoxy and make it more translucent and something that I could hold in my hands that made the glass and colored epoxy stand alone.

# Directions

1. Sprinkle the glass directly onto the plastic-wrapped Lazy Susan, leaving the center open. Try to keep all of the glass out of the center.

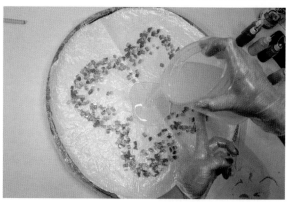

2. Pour the entire pint of epoxy into the center of the ring of glass.

3. Sprinkle more glass around the edges where the epoxy stopped spreading.

4. Lift and bunch up the plastic wrap from the sides of the Lazy Susan to create a barrier. This will allow the epoxy and glass to rest in a flower-like shape.

5. When you're satisfied with your plastic wrap round, wavy mold, drip your Alcohol iNK colors onto the uncured epoxy one color at a time.

## PRO TIP

- When working with glass, wear protective gloves and eye protection to avoid hurting yourself.

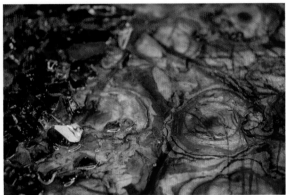

**6.** Create this unique geode-look by dripping your colors on top of each other in this pattern: blue-drop and allow it to expand; pink-drop and allow it to expand; gold-drop and allow it to expand; then pink-drop and allow it to expand. Make sure each new color is dropped in the same place.

**7.** Repeat this process and remember that the last color you dropped will fill in the center of the geode image.

**8.** Drip the colors over the glass as well.

**9.** You can add more glass around the edges, and it's okay if not all of it is touching the epoxy. You want the edges to be solid glass.

**10.** After you've allowed the epoxy to set halfway, which is about half the time of the manufacturer's directions, it's time to form the flexible epoxy over the form to create a bowl shape.

**11.** Lift the plastic wrap off the Lazy Susan, allowing any loose glass to fall away.

**12.** Turn the flexible epoxy creation upside down to drape over your plastic-wrapped form.

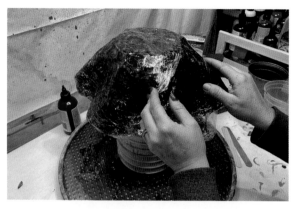

**13.** After your flexible epoxy creation is in its form, elevate it so none of the edges are touching the surface and it can drape freely.

**14.** Feel free to mold it and shape it so it looks like it was created by nature.

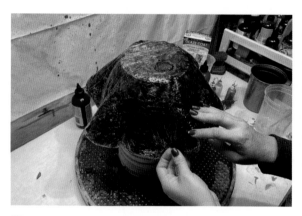

**15.** Several hours later, the flexible epoxy should be hardened. You can check it by knocking on it. If it seems hard enough, you can remove the plastic wrap and remove your piece from the form.

**16.** When you're certain that it is hardened, you can rinse with water to remove any of the dried Alcohol iNK from the glass.

## PRO TIPS

- A full cure can take up to 20 days. If the bowl isn't as open as you like, and you feel there is a small amount of flexibility, gently pry it open. Brace it using plastic household items that will fit snugly, but create the shape you want, and make the opening bigger. If it's too open, you can cinch it, bringing the sides closer, and brace it using electrical tape.
- Do not overdo the Alcohol iNK as it may inhibit your epoxy from curing.
- When working with epoxy, be sure to follow the manufacturer's safety recommendations.

# Neptune Chest

They don't make furniture today like they used to. Furniture from the early 1900s was built to be refinished: solid wood, heavy, and embellished with veneers of burl patterns. Fortunately, the bones tend to survive but not always the fragile veneers. Repairing veneer is something that I have yet to try. I have found a way to use Fluid Art on these old, chipped pieces and still be able to show off the beautiful areas of the burl veneer and hide the areas I repaired with wood filler. I feel that when I do fluid art on furniture, it makes the piece look as though it was carved out of a planet or a section of the sky.

With this dresser, I wanted to stain it one color to show off its bird's-eye maple veneer on the top and front of the drawers. Unfortunately, as I sanded it to the bare wood, it started chipping and flaking. I think it had been refinished once before and the veneer was worn too thin.

## What you'll need

- Unicorn SPiT colors: Weathered Daydream, Blue Thunder, and White Ning
- Gold mica powder
- Two large, clear plastic drop cloths
- Prepared piece of furniture (preferably sanded or stripped down to bare wood)
- Jumbo paintbrush
- Satin, oil-based topcoat
- Painter's tape
- Spray bottle of water

# Directions

1. Begin with a clean slate. Be sure any loose veneer has been removed and filled with FAMOWOOD Wood Filler and remove all drawers and set them aside. You're going to start with the top, so make sure that it's perfectly level.

2. Prepare the top by misting it with water, allowing the wood to become damp but not dripping. Apply lines of Blue Thunder, White Ning, and Weathered Daydream, creating a wave-like design. Be sure to use more White Ning than any other color to create multishades of dark colors.

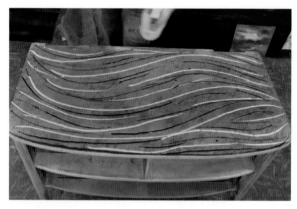

3. After you've laid out your colors, mist them with water, creating a saturated wet top. You should be able to see the pigments leach out from the colored stripes.

4. Place a piece of the clear plastic drop cloth over the top of the furniture. Be sure that the piece you cut is big enough to drape over all sides. When the plastic is down, mist the top with water.

5. Easily manipulate the colors and spread them out using your hands. The wet surface on the plastic should allow your hands to slip right across without moving the plastic. Stretch the colors following the same flow pattern that you created with color. Have fun manipulating the color until you feel the surface is fully covered. Just like Johnny B.!

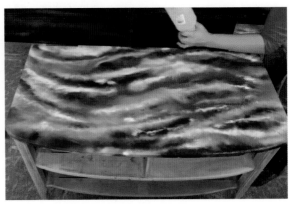

6. After stretching your colors, it's time for the reveal. To continue the flow, remove the plastic in the direction of the design.

7. To create a dramatic, cloud-like effect, mist lightly with water as you see fit.

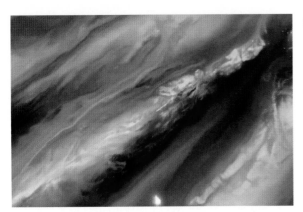

8. Be sure not to use too much water to keep from muddying the design much. It should look like this. While it's wet, feel free to sprinkle mica powder here and there as desired.

9. Also, don't be afraid that some of the natural tone of the wood might be showing through. That will add a three-dimensional effect once sealed. Allow it to dry naturally. Overnight should be enough time.

10. Now you're going to work on the drawers. Leaving the drawer face exposed, tape off the upper rim and sides to protect them.

11. Line up your drawers, face side up, in the same order as they will be when placed inside the dresser. Secure them together using painter's tape.

**12.** Apply the same stripes of colors and design as you did with the top. Cover with plastic and repeat the steps you did for the top. Allow each drawer to dry.

**13.** Mixing 3 parts White Ning and 1 part Weathered Daydream, stain the frame of the chest one solid color.

**14.** Mist your brush generously with water and keep your water bottle at hand so you can dilute as you go to achieve the coverage you like. Also, mist the wood with water so it will easily absorb the stain.

**15.** It's okay if your SPiT is not fully mixed, as it will create a multitonal effect that is beautiful. Simply dip your wet brush into the color, place your brush at the top, and pull down to the bottom in one long stroke.

**16.** Continue coloring the entire frame using long brushstrokes, following the flow of the grain until complete.

**17.** Once the design on your drawers is dry, separate them and stain the sides and interior of each drawer, if you like. I like to even stain the back if there are no maker's marks to give a finished look.

**PRO TIPS**

- I like to do the top and the drawers in the same session so they can dry at the same time and I can seal all of the parts at once.
- If your chest was a dresser and is missing the mirror, you could cut a piece of wood and create a backboard to fill the empty space as I did with this piece.

**18.** After the Unicorn SPiT is dry, you can seal the drawers using your favorite oil-based topcoat in gloss, satin, or matte.

**19.** I love to see the colors changing from the dark, rich tone from when they were wet to fading out to this chalky color. The magic happens when the topcoat goes on, making the colors come back to life in full vibrancy. Allow your topcoat to cure and you can Neptune-out your whole bedroom set if you like.

# Gemstone Side Table

## What you'll need

- Pouring medium mixed with White Ning, Zia, and Blue Thunder
- Concept color: Zeus
- Prepared side table
- Torch
- Disposable paper plate
- Large plastic cup
- Syringe
- Spray bottle of water
- Epoxy, like FAMOWOOD Glaze Coat

For inspiration on color palettes for my fluid art, I tend to look at polished gemstones like turquoise, marble, granites, and the more exotic stones. I like to see how they form and the natural colors that are in them. I choose my colors based on the stone that thrills me that day. This one happens to be a stone that's called Larimar. I love bringing natural elements into my home; the earth makes so many beautiful things. I find that a tabletop done like this is a piece of jewelry to decorate your home with.

I tilted my table to make my pigments flow in a way that replicated the veins and the growth pattern of this natural stone. Then I wanted to add strong gold veining. So, after the pour was complete and tilted to create my flow, I injected gold veining. I followed the edges that divided the colors with Zeus, to make prominent gold veining lines.

# Directions

1. Be sure that your tabletop is level and you have your pouring medium and colors prepared. Make a double batch of white. I used 1 part Unicorn SPiT to 5 parts pouring medium.

2. Pour your colors into the plastic cup and choose any pattern you like. I used the following color pattern: White Ning, Blue Thunder, Zia, Zeus; White Ning, Blue Thunder, Zia, Zeus, White Ning. Your results may be different from mine because flow art has its own mind.

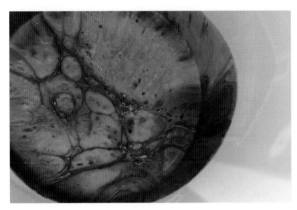

3. Look in your cup to see how beautiful the colors are!

4. Mist the top of your table generously with water.

5. Place the disposable cake plate on top of the cup and hold it tight with your hand.

6. Flip the cup over and set it on top of the table.

**7.** Hold the cup down and slip the plate out.

**8.** Poke a hole in the top of your cup, allowing air to enter. This will make your cup float. Create a trail of fluid color by sliding the cup around, focusing on the center.

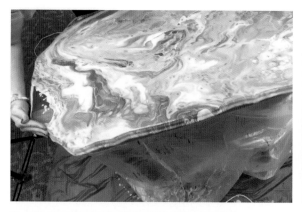

**9.** Once all your fluid has escaped the cup, you can tilt your table side to side, stretching the puddle to cover the entire surface. This will give you the natural stone resin look.

**10.** After the SPiT has settled, graze the surface with a flame to pop bubbles and create interesting cells. Now, fill a syringe with non-diluted Zeus and add veining if you like.

**11.** Allow it to dry overnight or up to 48 hours, depending on humidity. It will have a chalky-looking finish when it's dry. Mine only took 12 hours to dry because it was near my furnace room during winter.

**12.** To get a truly polished stone look, seal with epoxy.

## PRO TIPS

- Feel free to enhance and create the look of veining by injecting a small bead of the gold or any colors you want to make more prominent, following a design in the flow pattern. Do as much veining as you like, creating a natural effect like a real gemstone.

- Search online for pictures of stones that you like to get good ideas for color combinations.

- If the surface you are working on is stationary, use a hair dryer to direct the flow or to push the product around to cover the surface.

**13.** Be sure to also seal the sides by rubbing your gloved hand around the edges and a little under the lip to get that super-clean polished look. After the epoxy is fully cured, it will look like it was carved out of a real gemstone. You can gemstone your heart out on almost anything!

# Faux Labradorite Countertop

## What you'll need

- Unicorn SPiT colors: Blue Thunder, Navajo Jewel, Zia, Purple Hill Majesty, and Midnight's Blackness
- Thin drop cloth
- Painter's tape
- Degreasing agent
- 220-grit sandpaper
- Level
- Adhesive spreader
- Gloves
- FAMOWOOD Glaze Coat
- Spray bottles
- Spray bottle of water

Laminate countertops are durable, strong, and don't crack or break. Sometimes you may have to deal with some lifting. Replacing them with natural stone countertops can be very costly. I've seen people tint epoxy and do fluid art pours over their countertops. To me, that's too scary. That means that once you've poured it, it's on there. It's permanent and if you don't like it, you just threw away a lot of money because epoxy isn't cheap.

I've devised a way that you can color first to perfect your design. You can easily wash away an area you want to do again and then seal it to create polished stone-looking countertops on a budget with great ease and stunning results. I'll share the step-by-step process I used to transform laminate countertops into a labradorite masterpiece.

# Directions

1. Dilute your colors 1 part water to 3 parts Unicorn SPiT in spray bottles.

2. Make sure your surface is level. To prepare your surface, tape plastic drop cloths to the surfaces around and under your countertop. You don't want the Unicorn SPiT to spray all over the place. Protect your walls, cabinet, and floors.

3. Clean your surface with any type of degreaser.

4. Sand the surface with 220-grit sandpaper to make sure you get it deglossed so that it has some tooth.

5. You'll see variances with the spray bottle nozzle. If you turn the nozzle tight, it will give you a mist; if you open it completely, it will give you a streak. Mist the countertops in one direction. Natural stone grows in a pattern. Keep it in an organic flow by always spraying in an angled position, allowing the Unicorn SPiT to land like it's flowing.

## PRO TIPS

- If you have a surface-mount or an under-mount sink, it's best to remove them before doing your countertops. Also remove the faucet. Reinstall after the epoxy/resin has fully cured. This will give your countertops a more polished and professional look.

- If you're doing a countertop with a molded sink, like cultured marble, and no lip above, be sure to detach the drain and the faucet. This will allow the epoxy to continue to pour into the sink basin. Reinstall after the epoxy/resin has fully cured.

- If you would like to Unicorn SPiT your backsplash, you can cut boards that would fit perfectly. Don't forget to cut holes for the outlets. Lay them out level. Do the same process on the backsplash boards, then install them in place with panel glue.

- Take time to search online for images of stone to inspire your design.

- A little bit of Unicorn SPiT goes a very long way.

6. Create a patina color by using 1 part Dragon's Belly with 3 parts Zia. Dilute with 3 parts water.

7. Apply the patina color at an angle.

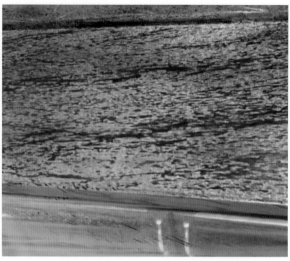

8. Open your spray bottle all the way. This will let you shoot bolts of color far away and close up.

9. Make one large line down the middle, just as you would imagine it would grow on its own.

10. Using your spray bottle, mist and spray the diluted Blue Thunder. Shake the bottle intermittently.

11. Next, apply diluted Navajo Jewel using the mist setting to keep the purple and blue colors bold. Remember to mist at an angle to maintain an organic flow.

12. Go over the colors with a fine mist of diluted Zia, a light turquoise color. This will give you some dimension.

13. The next layer is diluted Purple Hill Majesty. Spray that on to add a bold color.

14. Mist diluted Blue Thunder on top.

15. To top it off, mist diluted Midnight's Blackness. This is where you'll start to get the stone look. I like to add the black because it looks like little specks of another mineral coming through. Adding a little more will make it look like a vein running through. Go easy on the Midnight's Blackness though, it can overpower.

16. It's magic time! Take your bottle of water and mist above the counter without allowing it to change the flow direction. As you add the water, it will start to have a marbling effect. Go easy on the water though, you don't want it to muddy up too much.

17. If you're satisfied with the way it looks, let it dry. Remember, Unicorn SPiT is only permanent when you seal it. So, if you don't like the way it looks, you can wash it off and start over.

18. Paint the edges of the countertop a solid color.

19. You can let the color flow over the edges if you don't have a narrow concentrator attachment for your blow dryer. Tape a water bottle to a hair dryer so it has a direct area to flow. Aim the hair dryer in one direction. This will move the Unicorn SPiT and give it an organic shape. Wipe away and correct any areas you want to change. Allow to fully dry 3–24 hours depending on temperature and humidity.

20. When you're happy with your design and it's dry, you're ready to seal it. (Before you start, cover the floor, cabinets, and walls with plastic to protect them.) For this project, I made a gallon of FAMOWOOD Glaze Coat. It's always better to make more than enough to avoid bubbles, dimples, and separation. Be prepared to use the glaze coat right away since it hardens quickly. The box of epoxy always says what square footage it covers.

21. Start on one side and pour the sealant down the middle. What you'll notice about Unicorn SPiT is that it dries chalky. When you add epoxy, it gives it this bright, colorful appearance that it was when it was wet. Spread it out using an adhesive spreader. Don't go over an area more than three times. If you do, it's going to cause bubbles and dimples that you're going to have to sand and recoat. Allow it to go over your edges.

22. Smear any drips with your gloved hand.

23. Use a heat gun—I like to set mine at 980 degrees—or a butane torch. Pop all bubbles and make sure you don't overheat an area.

24. Let it set for an 90 minutes. Rub your gloved hand around the edges a few times to smooth any drips. Don't forget the area under the edges. If you miss any, you can use a sander or an Exacto knife to remove them.

25. Let it cure and harden for several days before placing heavy objects on it to avoid dents in your new polished countertops.

# CHAPTER TEN

# Furniture

You may be working with a brand-new piece that's bare wood and ready for your art. Or maybe you've found a piece with good bones that needs a little repair or have outdated furniture you inherited. I'm going to show you how to do some beautiful color-blending and give these household items, whether the piece is wood or not, a functional and artful afterlife.

When I talk about good bones, I mean a piece of furniture that is sturdy. You might want to put your hands on the top and move it front-to-back and side to side to make sure the legs aren't loose. Pull the drawers out to check the jointing to see if it's stapled or dovetailed. To be able to tell if something is wood or not, look at the back of the piece and the frame. I press my thumbnail in the same direction as the grain and scrape my fingernail up and down to see if it's soft like wood should be or if it's MDF (Medium Density Fiberboard), which is resin and sawdust.

When you're checking out the furniture, see if you can expose natural wood. Make sure the drawers pull out nicely. The real thing to look for is its weight. If something is light and wobbly, it will need structural work if you just can't pass it up.

# Tie-Dyed Organizer

### What you'll need

- Unicorn SPiT colors: White Ning, Zia, Lemon Kiss, Phoenix Fire, Pixie Punk Pink, Purple Hill Majesty, Navajo Jewel, and Blue Thunder
- E6000 Spray Adhesive
- Water
- Syringe
- Wax paper
- Resealable containers
- Rubber gloves
- Clear cling wrap
- Iron
- Finishing wax

Sometimes you just need to put all your stuff away in something small and compact that can fit pretty much anywhere. That's why this piece found a home with me. I needed a spot to stow my scarves, gloves, and winter hats. I knew this piece was the one because it was a blank slate. I was able to create an exciting piece by combining different techniques, from tie-dye to whitewashing to Sunset Press. It reminds me of the beautiful colors of the sunset, no matter what time of day it is. I found this little unfinished storage cart that I had to assemble. It made it easy to add color in a lot of different ways.

# Directions

1. The advantage of putting this cart together was that I could apply White Ning before assembling it. I used undiluted White Ning and covered all of the frame and the drawer hangers with it. After they dried, I sealed them with SPiT SHiNE Wax. This gave the wood a pickled effect.

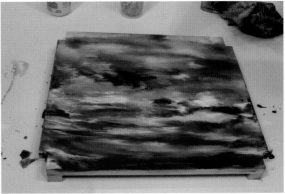

2. For the very top, I did the Sunset Stain Press (see Sunset Table project on page 248). I added Blue Thunder on both sides of the stain press so it would look like a sunset over an ocean.

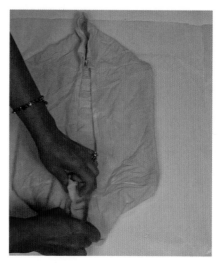

**3.** To prepare the canvas totes that connect to each drawer guide, I dipped them in water, making sure that they were completely soaked. Then I rang them out.

**4.** Put down some wax paper and lay down one wet canvas tote at a time. Fold each tote so that the bottom of the tote is lying flat on the wax paper. Fold the sides out to create a diamond and lay them flat on the wax paper, joining all of the trim pieces. Each one will be a different color, but of course, you can make them the same color and do them at the same time if you choose.

**5.** Make a mixture of E6000 Spray Adhesive and your desired colors into individual containers, creating a machine-washable fabric dye. The recipe I used is equal parts E6000 Spray Adhesive, Unicorn SPiT, and water.

**6.** Fill your syringe with your desired colors that flow together well on the color wheel (see page 3). Simply drizzle the color onto the fabric. I like to start with one color around the edges, another color going toward the middle, and a third color in the center. I also like to do small drips of the colors overlapping one another here and there.

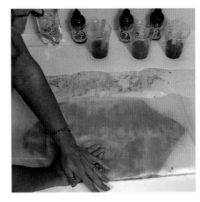

**7.** Take the wax paper and fold it over your color-saturated fabric and press down all around the top with your hand to squish the colors into the fabric. This makes it so the dye isn't just on the top but will saturate all the way to the bottom.

**8.** Pull back the wax paper to check out your work. If you feel you need more colorant, go ahead and add more, wrap it up, and squish it around again.

**9.** When you're satisfied with your colors, allow them to dry. You want to make sure they dry flat. If you're doing multiple colors, you'll want to separate them to avoid color transfer.

**10.** Once they are dry, give them a good rinse with cold water until the water runs clear. Allow them to dry again.

**11.** After the drawers are dry, preheat your iron at the appropriate setting for the type of fabric you have. Mine was set to canvas. When your iron is hot, iron out all those wrinkles.

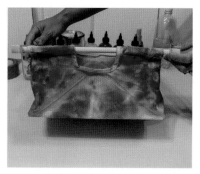  

**12.** Now they're ready to go back on their wooden drawer guides. When you touch the fabric, it may feel a little stiffer than before you colored it. If you want them to be softer, you can run them through your washing machine on the cold setting using laundry soap and fabric softener.

**13.** Now assemble as per the directions and enjoy.

## PRO TIPS

· The more water you use, the more pastel the colors will be.

· Don't be afraid to let the color of the fabric play a part in the design.

· The colors will show up better on white fabric. If the tote you find isn't white, bleach the fabric first to get the color as light as possible.

# Mariposa Live-Edge Table

I love wood grain, color, and the natural tones of some woods. Live edge has become so popular, it's not just for southwest decor or log homes anymore. Here I will show you my Mariposa technique for following the natural wood grain with a color pattern. In this project, I take a slab of kiln-dried white oak, add a zest of color, and embrace the natural tones of the wood. After it dries, I seal it organically, add a few modern hairpin legs, and create an organically modern hall table. This sets the stage to bring nature in its rawest form and the positivity of vibrant colors inside, to greet everyone who enters your home. This has become quite the conversation starter in my house.

## What you'll need

- Unicorn SPiT colors: SQUiRREL, Rustic Reality, Blue Thunder, and Navajo Jewel
- Slab of dried, live-edge white oak or similar light-toned wood
- Concept color: Athena
- Medium-size art brushes
- Spray bottle of water
- Orbital sander with 220-grit sandpaper
- Wire-brush drill attachment
- Rubber gloves
- SPiT SHiNE Wax
- Four hairpin table legs (or legs of your choice)

# Directions

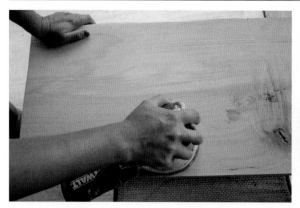

1. Use your sander to make the surface as smooth as possible, removing any blade marks. You can start with a higher grit of sandpaper to grind down any divots. Then use 220-grit sandpaper to make it smooth.

2. Use your wire-brush drill attachment to remove any bark from the live edge. After it's removed, finish with 220-grit sandpaper.

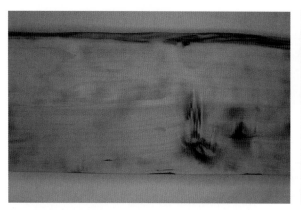

3. After your slab is smooth as a baby's bottom, dust it off, and wipe it down with a wet rag. Then you're ready to go.

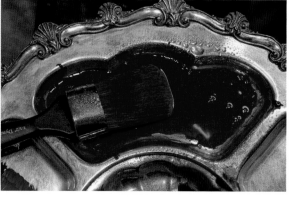

4. Pre-dilute your colors creating a wood dye. In separate containers, mix your colors using this formula: 1 part Unicorn SPiT to 5 parts water.

5. When looking at the way the grain is formed, select certain areas you want to highlight. I think knots in the wood are the perfect feature to show off. You can show these off by making them a beautiful electric blue. You're going to color it in and find the corresponding grain line that stretches across the entire board and follow it with your brush, creating a bolt of blue.

**6.** Now you have your line of interest, which in my piece of wood was the knot. Begin following the grain line in different colors going from Blue Thunder to Navajo Jewel to SQUiRREL. Then add Rustic Reality, and a line of undiluted Athena to maintain that bold, metallic punch.

**7.** Leave a strip of the natural wood tone for additional color and interest.

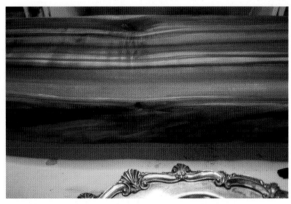

**8.** Follow the wood-grain pattern as it flows around the front, the back, and the sides for a realistic look as if the colors naturally grew within the wood.

**9.** On the live-edge side, you're going to get some elaborate grain pattern and I suggest you have fun with it.

**10.** After your design is dry, turn your piece over and lay it on a nonabrasive surface. Here you have the opportunity to give your color pattern another try, or you can stain it all one color like I did. I really love how the Blue Thunder picks up all the different tones in the wood, giving me turquoise, greens, and electric blue with just one color. It's fascinating and beautiful.

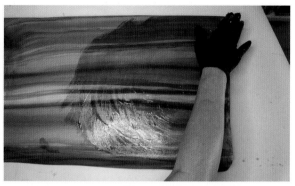

11. When your whole piece is dry, it's time to seal. Since it's such a large piece and the slab is very dry and very thirsty, it's going to need a lot of oil to cure and protect it.

12. Apply your SPiT Shine Wax or any penetrating oil directly onto the wood and spread out evenly.

13. These slabs of wood are so dry, that usually they'll soak up all the oil and will need between two to four applications.

14. Your final application can be applied using a wax brush with rapid circular motions until smooth and shiny. Or you can even use a buffing device if you have one.

15. After your live edge is sealed, it's time to give it some legs. Be sure to choose screws that are not so long that they will go all the way through the wood. It's also smart to predrill your holes before you secure the legs with screws. This will help you avoid cracks in the beautiful new focal point in your home.

## PRO TIPS

- Colors will be more vibrant on super-light or white-toned wood.
- Finding live-edge wood is very easy. Search online, including social media marketplaces, for slabs of live edge. You can also look for live edge pieces at your local woodcraft store.
- Barnwood sellers also offer live-wood pieces.

# Stylish Storage Cubby

Storage cubbies are widely available. They are very inexpensive and serve a great purpose with their individual slots for random items. I've turned this into an entertainment center for my son Joshua. Don't let laminated MDF turn you off if the function and price are right. I'm going to show you how to go over the existing plastic-like surface to give it a modern and contemporary finish that will turn this into the focal point of your family room.

## What you'll need

- Unicorn SPiT colors: Weathered Daydream and White Ning
- Sturdy MDF laminated storage cubby
- Pine board large enough to cover the top
- Piece of quarter round wood trim
- Torch
- Jumbo-size, flat paintbrush
- Hand saw to cut the cubby if you desire to make it smaller
- 120-grit sandpaper
- Oil-based, urethane in your preferred finish (matte, satin, or gloss)
- Large, synthetic fiber paintbrush
- Hair dryer
- E6000 Plus

# Directions for the pine-board top

1. If you want your storage cubby to be more of an entertainment console, simply saw off the first tier. Be sure to cut parallel to the top of the second tier to avoid any gaps. This is going to be the new top of your piece. This part will not be SPiTTED to make sure the new pine top will attach.

2. Once you've cut the cubby to desired size (you don't have to do that), thoroughly clean the surface with a degreaser and then rinse. Lightly sand the laminated surface with 120-grit sand-paper. This will give the laminate some tooth for the colorant to appear.

3. Add some drama to this piece by giving it a Shou Sugi Ban top. Using a butane torch, burn the surface of the pine board. You will see that the grains in the pine will become very dark. Make sure you burn the wood evenly and avoid making a cheetah print. It's important to burn following the grain. If you do end up with cheetah prints when you burn, feel free to burn a little more until they blend in. It's a good idea to do this step outside and to follow all fire safety guidelines.

4. After you've burned it as even as you can get it, sand the toasted surface with 120-grit sand-paper, following the flow of the grain. Remove any char, but leave behind the shadow of the burn, which will make it look like zebra-striped wood. It's okay if you have a few cheetah prints. I can't ever get it perfect.

5. Mist the pine board with water because it's time to stain.

**6.** Apply a 1-inch-wide bead of White Ning across the end of the pine board. Then, add half-inch drops of Weathered Daydream on top of the White Ning, 1 inch apart. Wet your brush with water and drag the brush through the strip of SPIT across the board, all the way to the other end. Do as many of these brushstrokes as needed to spread the color evenly across the top. Add as much or as little as you need until the top is covered in these stripes of stain.

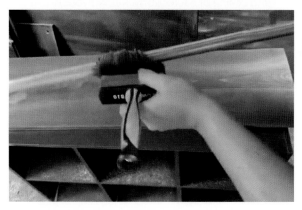

**7.** Use the excess stain in your brush to color the quarter round. Let it dry.

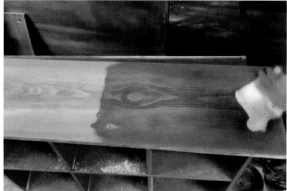

**8.** If you feel that you've applied too much stain and it looks more like paint, use a damp rag to remove excess stain. This will reveal a more pronounced grain pattern. Set your board aside and allow it to dry.

## Directions for the laminated base

**1.** If you want to color the bottom, turn the unit upside down before you start.

### PRO TIPS

- For a super-finished look, be sure to paint each cubby this way: top, bottom, and both sides.
- Make sure the MDF is clean. When you sand, you want to do what's called "deglossing" to remove any shine. When cleaning the MDF, steel wool will also help with the deglossing process.

**2.** To continue this simple blending pattern, add a 1-inch bead of White Ning and drops of Weathered Daydream 1 inch apart on the sides. There's no need to put the colors on a palette first. Feel free to apply the colors to the tip of your brush. Remember, if you cut the top off your cubby there's no need to paint the exposed MDF or laminate.

**3.** Simply place your loaded brush into the inside corners where the side meets the shelf and pull straight up, covering the sides one single brushstroke at a time. Repeat to do the shelf and ceiling of each cubby. Reload your brush as needed.

**4.** Dry using your hair dryer on high heat.

**5.** After it dries, use a synthetic brush to seal with urethane. Apply the urethane in thin coats. Your brushstrokes should follow the design pattern. Apply two to three coats, allowing the urethane to dry in between.

**6.** When the urethane on the base is dry, attach the quarter round trim piece to the pine board using nails or glue. Then adhere the new top to the bare laminate using E6000 Plus.

**7.** Seal the pine board and quarter round with urethane, like the base, or your preferred oil-based topcoat.

# Poppy Flower Table

Vintage or antique side tables can be found just about anywhere: garage sales, estate sales, and even online swap and shops. They can add an artsy pizazz to any little nook of your house. For this project, Holly McAnlis, one of our online forum members, will show you how she utilized the beautiful grain lines in the wood grain to create the delicate veins in flower petals. Holly has been able to profit during retirement doing what she loves and enjoys while recycling outdated furniture and bringing art into many homes.

## What you'll need

- Unicorn SPiT colors: Molly Red Pepper, Rustic Reality, Midnight's Blackness, Phoenix Fire, and White Ning
- Small table
- Styrofoam plate
- Painter's brush
- 220-grit sandpaper
- Chalk paint
- Pencil

# Directions

1. Strip and sand the top of your piece to the bare wood using an orbital sander. I always finish by hand-sanding with 220-grit sandpaper. Clean the base and cover it with chalk paint.

2. Use a pencil to lightly draw the image you plan to stain.

3. Use a thin coat of clear oil-based sealer on the whole top as a wood conditioner before applying Unicorn SPiT. I like how my Unicorn SPiT goes on over tinted oil stains too.

   **NOTE:** You can get this without having to sand an existing clear coat off 100 percent. Then there is no need for additonal sealer.

4. Use a Styrofoam plate as your color palette when blending Unicorn SPiT with water. A paper plate will not last and will soak up your Unicorn SPiT. Place Molly Red Pepper generously on the plate. Then, use a brush and dip it in the water to dilute the color so you can outline over your pencil marks and make your image easier to view.

 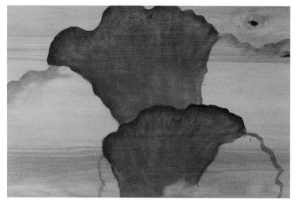

5. Go back around the edges, laying red and then pulling it down from the edge. Use Molly Red Pepper and a larger brush with a clean shop cloth on your finger to fill in all the petals. Dunk a brush in the water, mix it with the Molly Red Pepper on the plate, and begin laying the color into each petal.

6. Using a dab of Midnight's Blackness, mix in a small amount of Molly Red Pepper to make a merlot color that you can use as detail and contrast in areas.

7. Continue to use the darker shades to accentuate depth in areas. Lay the SPiT with a brush, and then blend it with your finger wrapped in a shop cloth.

**NOTE:** This is a picture of the progress I've made from the above steps.

8.  Add Phoenix Fire to highlight and give your project interest. Use a brush with water on some areas and full strength on other areas. Pull the color around to blend and adjust as you go.

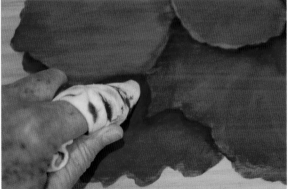

9.  Create more contrast and depth, and get more details, by adding Rustic Reality to small areas. I also use a pre-tinted, dark walnut oil-based stain to allow me to lay the dark areas without wiping the SPiT away.

**10.** You can outline the petals in white using a brush and a rag. (This step was a last-minute adjustment.) I wasn't happy with the results, so I played with this for quite a while. I think next time I would leave the white out of this piece and just stay with the dark details. I continued to mess with the white and dark details until I was satisfied.

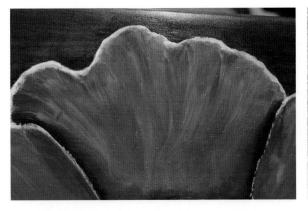 

**11.** Apply Phoenix Fire and pull it through with your gloved finger. This will give it a more vibrant highlight.

**12.** Take the piece outside and give it a coat of gloss lacquer to seal your Unicorn SPiT. Lacquer should not be sprayed indoors due to high fumes, but it dries fast and then you can bring it back inside.

## PRO TIP

· A water-based topcoat and sealer can be used indoors if you are not sensitive to it. It has a low fume smell and dries quickly. You can use a water-based sealer with Unicorn SPiT as long as you seal it first with a couple coats of oil-based topcoat. You can seal with a beeswax-based sealing wax first, but you will have to let it cure 100 percent before applying a water-based topcoat.

 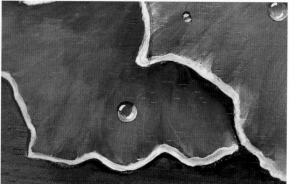

**13.** To apply dew drops on the petals, put Midnight's Blackness and White Ning on your plate. You can dilute it or use it at full strength. With a fine brush, make a half-circle on top with Midnight's Blackness and blend it into the center a little. You don't want to cover the whole inside of the circle. Then do the bottom half with White Ning and smudge it up toward the center. You can use a Q-tip or a small smudging stump to get the blending right. Remember, you are applying over sealed SPiT, so if you don't like one of your dew drops, just wipe it off with a wet paper towel and start again. To finish the droplets, apply a white strip at the top and opposite bottom of the circle, leaving the center clear. Once you're happy with the dew drops, seal it again with lacquer.

**14.** Give the small basket drawer a wash of very diluted Molly Red Pepper over the entire drawer. Take a new knob and use Unicorn SPiT to match the art on the top. Seal everything with lacquer. Seal the top art with three coats of a water-based topcoat over two coats of lacquer, or just keep oil-based if you like. Sand or buff with 220-grit sandpaper in between each coat of sealer.

**15.** These pictures are of the finished project. The base is black chalk paint. It took me two days to complete this piece from sanding, cleaning, chalk painting, art, and finish.

# From MDF to OMG Chest

French Revival used to be all the rage. You can find gorgeous pieces of furniture with magnificent architectural detail formed out of a plastic-resin-like substance, mingled with MDF paneling. Laminate was also popular due to its durability, so you will find a lot of the tops on these pieces are faux wood—a hard laminate that looks like wood grain. In the 1980s and '90s, these pieces of furniture were made to last. They are heavy, sturdy, and have the perfect bones to create a magnificent canvas. We're going to take this outdated chest and give it a beautiful farmhouse look with a weathered barnwood top.

## What you'll need

- Unicorn SPiT colors: Rustic Reality, Midnight's Blackness, White Ning, and Weathered Daydream
- Concept color: Athena
- Liquid wood canvas concoction (see page 3)
- Stir stick
- Jumbo flat artist brushes
- Spray bottle of water
- Silicone grain pattern curve tool
- Shop cloth
- Sanding block
- Paint palette
- Satin or matte oil-based topcoat
- Silver spray paint
- Tiny spray bottle

223

# Directions for faux barnwood top

1. Create a prepared surface by thoroughly cleaning all surfaces with a degreasing agent, and then rinse. Remove all metal hardware. Clean those, too.

2. Make enough liquid-wood canvas concoction to cover the entire chest: front, sides, and top. You can make all of it at once, or as you go.

3. Tint your liquid-wood canvas gray, by mixing in a little Midnight's Blackness. You can make it as dark or as light as you wish. Tint to your taste, but remember that you can't ever make it a vibrant color. It will always be a pastel.

4. Pour big globs of the liquid-wood canvas on top of the piece.

5. Use your jumbo brush to spread the concoction easily across the entire top. Use long brushstrokes, creating your first element of faux wood grain. Your brushstrokes are very important here as they will be part of your design. Be sure to wash out your brush immediately, as this concoction will damage your brush if it dries. You can also submerge your brushes in a cup of water to clean later.

6. Using a silicone grain-pattern curve tool, drag it through the wet surface. Rock and pivot the tool while dragging to simulate a grain-and-knot plank design. This may take some practice, but you can apply more of your liquid-wood canvas concoction, smooth with the brush, and try over and over again.

7. Apply a base coat of the liquid-wood canvas concoction to the front and sides of the base of the chest. Remember to use flattering brushstrokes that go with the flow of the architecture.

8. After the top is dry, you can color your planks of wood. Load your paint palette with Rustic Reality, White Ning, and Weathered Daydream. Line up your colors with one another, wide enough to be able to triple-load your jumbo brush with all three colors. You're going to stagger your 1½-foot brushstrokes to create the look of a wood-plank floor.

9. If you want to blend like I did, simply mist with water and blend using a damp, large clean brush.

10. Allow it to dry and seal with one coat of oil-based topcoat.

**11.** After the topcoat is fully cured, use a fine-grit sanding block to lightly sand the raised edges formed by your graining tool. This will expose only the top edges of the liquid wood canvas, making them porous. Once complete, dry-dust off.

**12.** Wrap your sanding block with a clean, damp shop cloth.

**13.** Apply a small amount of Midnight's Blackness to the cloth and rub it around, creating an ink pad. Not dripping wet, just dampened with the Midnight's Blackness.

**14.** Very lightly, skim your makeshift ink pad across the top, following the grain. This will stain that newly exposed liquid-wood canvas, giving it a realistic, weathered wood look.

**15.** This will complete your faux-weathered barn-wood top. You just need to seal it with your preferred oil-based topcoat. I chose a satin finish and did three coats.

# It's all about the base

1. Continuing your weathered barnwood look, double-load a flat jumbo brush with Weathered Daydream and Rustic Reality. Create vertical stripes on all flat surfaces.

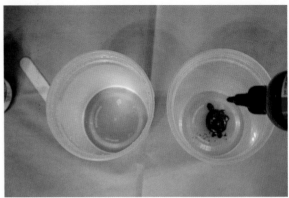

2. Mix a bit of Weathered Daydream and Rustic Reality with some water.

3. Color wash over the other areas, like the architectural detail, to give them a little pop of color. You can go as dark with it as you like.

4. You can also blend White Ning and Rustic Reality with a double-loaded brush on all drawer and door inserts. Once it's dry, give it one coat of oil-based topcoat in the finish of our choice.

5. After the gray is sealed, load a brush with Athena and work it into all crevices.

6. After you apply Athena, wipe with a damp cloth to remove the copper color from any raised areas, exposing the gray.

7. Load a sponge brush with Mercury and drag it, grazing the top edges of the architectural detail to add a bit of a silver glow.

8. Seal with two coats of satin, oil-based topcoat.

# Let's tinker-up the hardware

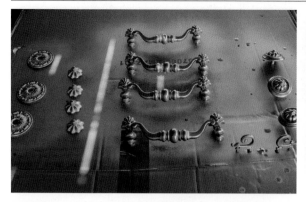

**1.** Once your hardware is thoroughly cleaned, apply silver spray paint and allow it to cure.

**2.** Make a mix of 1 part Midnight's Blackness to 5 parts water in your tiny spray bottle and shake it up.

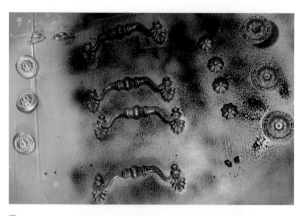

**3.** Mist all silver hardware with the Midnight's Blackness wash to create little black speckles and allow to dry.

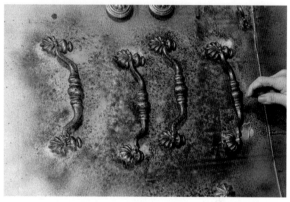

**4.** Mix 1 part Zeus to 3 parts water in a tiny spray bottle and mist the hardware, creating gold speckles. Allow it to dry and seal with a satin aerosol spray topcoat.

**5.** Put your hardware back on and you're all done.

## PRO TIPS

- If you want to create an extra layer to show off the architectural details, you can glaze with Midnight's Blackness around the inserts of the drawers after they are sealed. Do this before you do the copper.

- Sealing each step as you go creates depth in the piece. But these added layers of sealant also add durability. If you choose to use wax to seal the layers, you will have to allow it to fully cure, which can take days. That's why I choose to seal my layers with urethane—it cures enough for the next step in only a few hours.

# CHAPTER ELEVEN

# Signature Techniques

The Signature techniques you're going to find in this chapter are mostly ones I discovered while trying to tap into the creativity of those who are physically and/or mentally disabled. You're going to find that these techniques are so easy and meaningful that they will surely become your favorites. We will cover the Aura, the Galaxy, the Sunset, and the old-world distressing technique I created called Caribbean and Crimson Color Washing. You will find that no matter your artistic level or physical capabilities, you will be able to apply these techniques on any substrate that you feel has good bones. (**NOTE:** These techniques are what grabbed people's attention and started the Unicorn SPiT movement.)

# Crimson Color Wash Wine Caddy

Boxed wine is making a comeback. I've always enjoyed some Franzia, but recently I've noticed that there are some higher-quality wines readily available in a box. This is awesome because it extends the life of the wine by not exposing it to oxygen. The one drawback is the stigma that box wine has. So, for

social gatherings, wedding receptions, and parties, I've designed a tasteful solution that also lets you release your artistic side. You won't be ashamed to display this boxed-wine caddy on your bar or kitchen counter.

## What you'll need

- Unicorn SPiT color: Midnight's Blackness
- Concept color: Zeus
- Clean cloth
- Vinyl glove
- Paper plate
- Large spray bottle
- Small spray bottle
- Chip brush
- Flat brush

## After the wood dries, you'll need

- A shot glass
- SPiT SHiNE
- Waxing brush
- PiNCH Powder
- Square container
- Unicorn SPiT colors in Midnight's Blackness and concept color Zeus
- Screen stencil
- Business card to use as a scraper

# Directions

1. Sand imperfections with a sanding block.

2. Create a cranberry color by mixing Midnight's Blackness with Molly Red Pepper. Mix the cranberry color with water-based topcoat. Brush the mixture on one panel at a time. Brush on an even coat. Wipe it off before it is completely dry.

3. Rub SPiT Shine Wax on the two edges of the door panel and let them dry. This allows the door to slide open and close easily.

4. When dry, reassemble the wine box.

5. Pour Midnight's Blackness and Zeus separately on the box, allowing them to drip to the bottom.

## PRO TIP

- Be sloppy and apply liberally.

**6.** Take a flat brush and pull the colors downward toward the bottom.

**7.** Once the Midnight's Blackness and Zeus have been stretched out vertically, covering the cranberry color, add a bead of Zeus at the top and allow it to drip down.

**8.** Once gravity has taken hold of the bead of Zeus, mist with water, allowing the Zeus to further melt and also reveal some of the cranberry color that's underneath. Repeat these steps for all sides of the box.

**9.** After your Unicorn SPiT has dried, use a damp cloth to wipe away some of the Zeus and Midnight's Blackness to reveal more of the cranberry color, if desired.

**10.** You can Apply Zeus to your fingers and flick small amounts, concentrating on the top and very little on the bottom. If the flicks turn out too big, mist lightly with water. Only do this if you want more gold.

**11.** Allow it to dry.

## PRO TIP

· Don't be afraid to let some of the cranberry color peek through when wet-distressing with your spray bottle of water.

# Stenciling and Sealing

1. In a resealable container, mix 1 oz. of Poseidon with three spoonfuls of PiNCH Powder. Stir well, put the lid on, and allow it to develop for 20 minutes. Once developed, stir again to create a fluffy, smooth paste.

2. Lightly apply the screen stencil anywhere on the box.

3. Apply a small amount of the developed PiNCH Powder with a scraper—a business card will work—over the top of the screen stencil. Listen for a sound like a record scratching. Cover the area of the stencil, being careful to stay within the area of the stencil. Apply the screen stencil lightly to your dry surface and "scrape on" your stencil paste onto the stencil surface. Use a minimal amount. There's no need to cake it on. Peel off the stencil and repeat in other areas if desired.

4. Peel off the screen stencil and repeat in other areas if desired. Depending on your preference, use a sanding block and sand the stencil lightly to create a distressed look. Do not sand if you want a bright image.

**5.** Seal with SPiT SHiNE or your preferred oil-based topcoat.

# Hummingbird Aura

I discovered the Aura technique by placing a board in front of the folks at the day-care center and asking them what colors they were feeling that day. Then I would lay those colors out one at a time for them to spread out. I feel this really freed them. They didn't even need a brush! You can start by sanding down the bare wood if you're refinishing, or you can begin with a freshly primed surface as I did for this one. This top had several cracks in it, so I filled them in and primed it with my liquid-wood canvas concoction. You want to keep in mind that you want to use the colors that correspond with the color wheel (page 3).

## What you'll need

- Unicorn SPiT colors: Blue Thunder and Zia
- Concept colors: DiONYSUS, Poseidon, Zeus, and Atlantis
- Prepared flat and solid surface
- Spray bottle of water
- Jumbo flat artist brushes
- Gloves
- Hair dryer
- Shop cloth
- Aerosol clear coat
- Oil-based topcoat of your choice and finish
- Scrub brush

# Directions

1. For this project, you can sand down to the bare wood or over an existing finish. I wanted mine to be nice and bright so I gave it a coat of my liquid wood concoction and allowed it to cure. Once cured, mist the surface.

2. Create rainbow bands of the colors of your choice, making sure to put the lightest color in between each band, as I did with the Zia in this photo.

3. Place your gloved hand in the middle of the rainbow and slide it outward, moving the pigment in a blazing pattern. This will give you a tie-dyed look.

4. The most wonderful thing about Unicorn SPiT is if you don't like what you see, or change your mind midstream, you can redo it. Simply take a wet shop cloth and wipe away excess. You can even wash it away if it has dried. The residual color will still be present in an unsealed or porous surface.

**5.** Now that the excess is removed, I'm going for my Aura Blast technique. Do this one-color layer at a time, laying your first color bead starting farthest out from the center.

**6.** Starting from the middle of the top of your art, slide your hand inward, following the arch all the way around the surface. Always end with your hand in the middle. That will give us our base tone. The color I used was DiONYSUS.

**7.** Use a damp cloth to remove excess, creating a half-moon shape almost to the edges, but not all the way.

**8.** On your newly cleaned-off radius, apply a bead of Blue Thunder, following the radius a few inches in.

**9.** Use your gloved hands to smear the bead of Blue Thunder outward to the edges using your fingers to create a feather-like design.

**10.** You can spread the color out as much or as little as you desire, but be sure you do not completely cover the DiONYSUS as this will be your second layer of blazing color.

**11.** Use a cloth to wipe away excess in a radius a bit smaller than the previously cleaned radius.

**12.** Apply a bead of Atlantis in the semi-circle design.

**13.** Use your gloved fingers as your brush to slide through the pigment to create thin, feather-like designs. Be sure to start in the middle and work your way around the semicircle. Don't completely cover the Blue Thunder as this will be your third layer. If your color is not as strong as you would like, repeat the same process in the same placement.

**14.** You're going to clear a semicircle with a damp rag, removing the excess. Make sure that when creating a new layer, your radius should get smaller and smaller as you go.

## PRO TIP

· When doing your aura, make sure you alternate between light and dark colors. This helps to create the layering, giving it a lot of depth.

**15.** Make a semicircle bead of Zia. As you can see, our semicircle beads are getting smaller and smaller as we go.

**16.** Use your palm to create fatter feather designs, but do not completely cover the Atlantis. This will be your fourth layer.

**17.** When your Zia is stretched out to your desire, clean another semicircle that's smaller than the prior semicircle.

**18.** Create a semi-radius bead of Poseidon and feather out that design. If it seems too prominent, feel free to wipe some off and feather out any residual into the Zia.

**19.** Clean the center again and apply a bead of DiONYSUS.

**20.** Using a small, flat cylinder paintbrush, you can feather the DiONYSUS into a radius for a softer look. Be sure not to fully color the Poseidon and Zia layer. This will create layer number five. If it becomes dry, you can wet your brush with water to reactivate the pigment and blend.

**21.** Now that your radiuses are getting very small, it's time to create the aura's crown. After you clear a small semicircle, apply a bead of Zeus.

**22.** Slide your hand through the bead of gold, reaching out over the purple, but do not fully cover it. This will create layer number six.

**23.** Create another small semicircle. Apply a bead of Blue Thunder and stretch it over the Zeus, creating layer number eight. Blend out as much as you desire.

**24.** Closing your crown, clear a very small semicircle using Blue Thunder. Apply Zia and use your fingers to stretch the Zia over the Blue Thunder, but not totally covering it.

**25.** I like to use my base color as my closing color. I feel that it brings the image full circle. There's no need to clear a semicircle. Just add a small drop to the center and use your fingers, or brush to fan out your final and ninth layer. You don't have to do nine layers like I did. You can do as many as you want, but the more layers, the more dimension.

### PRO TIP

· Don't be afraid to do a layer of the natural tone of the wood. That will give it a great three-dimensional look when you seal it with epoxy.

**26.** Dry it using a hair dryer, or leave it overnight, whichever you have time for. Then spray a coat of clear sealant to lock it down in preparation for highlighting. I do this to protect my design from being reactivated by my highlighting colors. If you're satisfied with how it looks, then you're finished. Or you can add highlights or lowlights after the first coat of sealant is applied, protecting your original design.

**27.** Now that the original design is protected, you can add colors straight to the brush or put some color on a palette.

**28.** Add your highlight and lowlight colors using the side of your brush in soft and airy brush-strokes. Following the design layers, create small, feather-like designs here and there. Always aim toward the center.

**29.** Do these feather-like strokes, intensifying any of the color bands that you wish.

**30.** If you feel that you did not achieve the softness you want, feel free to glaze over the surface. Starting in the middle and working your way out, follow the semicircle pattern with the dry scrub brush.

**31.** Not all auras will need this. It's up to you.

**32.** If the SPiT has dripped onto the base of your project and it's already sealed, you can easily clean off any drips or smudges with a cloth and a little water.

**33.** It's time to color the edge of your piece, creating a beautiful frame for your aura. I chose an oil-based gold. From here you seal your project with your prefered oil based topcoat.

# Galaxy Chair

I've always been fascinated with the stars at night. I get mesmerized by looking at the photos NASA releases of far-off galaxies and nebulas. It makes you think of the great unknown and realize the universe is endless, just like our imagination. This Galaxy Stain Press allows you to choose colors from your imagination, or from NASA's beautiful photos, and apply them to everyday items. This will create a feeling of endless possibilities that can captivate your imagination and satisfy astronomers, Star Wars fans, and regular-old people like us.

## What you'll need

- Unicorn SPiT color: Midnight's Blackness, Zia, Blue Thunder, Purple Hill Majesty
- Chair with wooden seat
- Plastic drop cloth (cut to about three inches larger than your surface)
- Spray bottle of water
- FAMOWOOD Glaze Coat

# Directions

1. Set up your workspace on a level surface. On the bare-wood side of your seat, apply Unicorn SPiT (Zia, Blue Thunder, and Purple Hill Majesty) in a spiral pattern and mist with water. What I liked about the IKEA chair was how one side of the seat was bare wood and the other was stained and sealed.

2. Lay your plastic drop cloth over your seat and allow it to suction down on its own as much as possible. Tug on the corners and the sides, pulling it tight to get rid of any wrinkles or bubbles.

3. After your plastic is on, mist the top with water to make it slick for your gloved hand to glide across it. Start in the middle and slide your hand out, spreading the Unicorn SPiT to the edges. You will see a tie-dye pattern evolve.

4. With your pattern on and your surface covered in Unicorn SPiT, all you have to do is grab the corners and lift the drop cloth, revealing the center last. In doing so, you cause the Unicorn SPiT to flow in a movement that looks like it's shooting inward.

5. After your tie-dye pattern is down, put a bit of Midnight's Blackness on your fingertips and flick the SPiT onto your design from a distance. Repeat the flicking with Zia, then mist with water. When you mist these little flicks, it turns them into shooting stars and meteors! Let it dry. (**NOTE:** Unicorn SPiT dries to a chalky finish, but once sealed with any oil-based sealer, it turns as vibrant as it was when it was wet.)

6. Now, it's time to seal the seat with FAMOWOOD Glaze Coat. This stuff is super durable. It's water-resistant and heat resistant up to 120 degrees Fahrenheit, is hard as a rock, and looks like glass. One coat is equal to 70 coats of varnish. I knew it was the best choice for my rough-and-tough boys.

7. Let the seat dry overnight to a rock-hard, glass-like finish. Mine had a couple of little drips on the underside, so I sanded them down with my sander and started the assembly. The IKEA chair included everything I needed to put the frame together. Every little wooden dowel, screw, and even a little crank tool came in the box. You will need a Phillips screwdriver to secure the seat to the frame.

## PRO TIP

- The KAUSTBY chair went together so easily. It took me about 10 minutes from beginning to end. The quality of this chair is just crazy great! It's super sturdy, there's a nice weight to it, and it's very modern.

# Sunset Table

## What you'll need

- Unicorn SPiT colors: White Ning, Zia, Blue Thunder, Pixie Punk Pink, Phoenix Fire, Midnight's Blackness, and Lemon Kiss
- Spray bottle of water
- Thin, clear plastic drop cloth big enough to cover the entire surface
- Projector
- Epoxy, like FAMOWOOD Glaze Coat
- Heat gun or flame
- Plastic adhesive spreader

It's always fun to capture silhouettes of wildlife, mountains, or children at play—to trap time in a bottle. Growing up in New Mexico, we lived in the middle of the desert. From as far back as I can remember, it was almost a daily delight to go outside at sunset and witness the sun laying down to rest on our beautiful horizon. It enchanted us with its beautiful colors. The pinks, reds, turquoise, and blues, with hints of orange and gold-lined clouds always let me know that tomorrow I would wake up to the same beauty, but on the other side. The sunset was a constant reminder that tomorrow would be a brand-new day and that I could rest easy, knowing that everything was going to be all right.

# Directions

1. I found this table on the side of the road. It was filthy and the laminated top was cracked, so I removed the top and cleaned the bottom.

2. To create a new top, measure, cut, and router the edges of a piece of 1-inch oak plywood. If you're going with a vertical design, cut with the grain running top to bottom. If you're going for a long flow like the sky, cut the board with the grain running horizontally. I chose horizontal for this piece.

3. After the wood has been cut to size and the sides of the board have been sanded smooth, you are ready to begin. Condition the dry wood by misting it liberally with water.

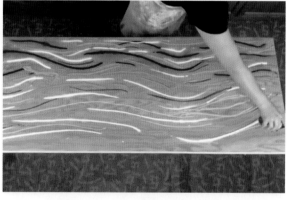

4. To create a sky, add flowing beads of color in a wave-like pattern. White Ning should be placed from top to bottom equally. Phoenix Fire and Pixie Punk Pink should be concentrated at the bottom. Gradually add fewer and fewer beads as you reach the top. Add beads of Blue Thunder and Zia, concentrating at the upper edge. Add beads of Lemon Kiss, concentrating on the center. Be sure not to get the Lemon Kiss too close to any of your blue lines because that will create green, which is fine if you're trying to create a tornado look.

## PRO TIP

· After your stain press is dry on bare wood, the grain may be raised. You can tell if it has been raised because you can feel fibers sticking up like stubby hairs. Gently buff the surface with a clean piece of cardboard with light pressure until it's smooth. Frequently change out your cardboard to a fresh piece to avoid color transfer.

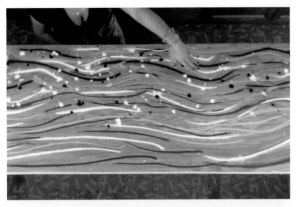

**5.** Sprinkle dots of White Ning here and there over and around the blue areas. Then, add small drops of Blue Thunder here and there with a few drops overlapping into the Pixie Punk Pink, Lemon Kiss, and Phoenix Fire. A bead or two of Zia can also be added to the very bottom, along with the orange and pink.

**6.** Now that all your colors are laid down, mist liberally with water again.

**7.** Place your precut piece of clear drop cloth over your work. Try to avoid wrinkles. The plastic will appear to vacuum-seal down. It's fun to watch. You don't have to worry about small bubbles, but try to lift the drop cloth to release any giant bubbles.

**8.** After the plastic is laid on top of the colors, it's time to spread them around with your gloved hands. Simply spray the plastic with water to be able to slide your hands around freely without tugging or shifting the plastic.

**9.** If you feel that you need more color in a certain area, just lift the plastic drop cloth and squirt a few more beads of color. I felt that I needed more Blue Thunder and White Ning.

**10.** Place the plastic cloth back down and continue to move the color around, smearing it in the same flow pattern as you placed your beads of color.

**11.** Once the colors have been stretched out to cover the entire surface, peel the drop cloth off while your pigments are still wet, pulling the drop cloth off in the same direction as your flow pattern.

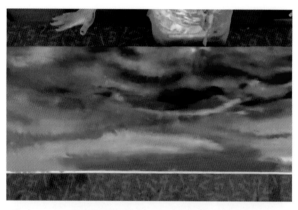

## PRO TIP

- You can make this either a sunrise or a sunset, depending on which side you place your silhouette. For a sunset, place your silhouette over the orange, yellow, and pink side. For a sunrise, place your silhouette over the blue side. Or you can allow your artwork to decide and place your silhouette on the side that looks best.

**12.** Let your work dry on a level surface. Feel free to tip your tabletop side to side to enhance the flow if desired.

**13.** After the top is dry, set it vertically and project your desired image. For mine, I traced some horse silhouettes on a clear projector sheet.

**14.** Using a wet artist brush, apply Midnight's Blackness, filling in the silhouette design. Don't worry about brushstrokes as they will disappear when you seal.

**15.** When dry, lay your piece on an elevated level surface. Make sure to protect your floors and make sure that all of the edges are freestanding. Remember to tape off any base that it's attached to or standing on. Pour your epoxy down the middle of your artwork from side to side to make sure you have an even amount to spread out.

**16.** Use a plastic adhesive spreader to grab the epoxy puddle and pull it out to the edges. Be careful not to scratch the surface. You want to do this gently, like frosting a cake. Allow the epoxy to run over the sides if you have enough to spare. Generally, a quart will cover 6½ square feet.

**17.** Fan over the surface with a heat source, like a heat gun or flame, to pop any bubbles. Be careful not to overheat, scorch, or boil.

**18.** Allow your epoxy to cure, and enjoy this beautiful, three-dimensional effect you can't achieve with any other art medium in the world.

# Caribbean Color Wash Wine Caddy

Bermuda, Bahama, come on, pretty mama. When you go to the coast, whether it's east or west, it's wonderful to walk the shores and find little treasures. There are thousands of undiscovered, buried treasures. You can find gold coins, washed-up pieces of wood from ancient shipwrecks, and pieces of sea glass, too. I created this style to fulfill the excitement a treasure hunter must feel or how I would feel to be lucky enough to have a real treasure box wash up on shore, right at my feet. This piece makes me feel adventurous and reminds me of my world travels.

## What you'll need

- Mahogany self-sealing stain (see color wheel page 3—red and black)
- Concept color: Zeus
- Unicorn SPiT colors: Blue Thunder and Zia
- Same color as stencil
- Clean cloth
- Vinyl glove
- Paper plate
- Large spray bottle
- Small spray bottle
- Chip brush
- Flat brush

## After the wood dries, you'll need

- SPiT SHiNE Wax
- Waxing brush
- PiNCH Powder
- Square container
- Unicorn SPiT colors in Midnight's Blackness and concept color Athena (copper)
- Screen stencil
- Business card to use as scraper

## Directions

1. Sand imperfections with a sanding block.

2. Mix custom mahogany color (1 part Midnight's Blackness and 3 parts Molly Red Pepper) with 30 parts water-based top coat.

3. Use the Unicorn SPiT custom mahogany color and water-based topcoat mixture to brush onto the surface, one panel at a time. Wipe on an even coat. Wipe it off before it's completely dry.

4. Rub SPiT SHiNE on the two edges of the door panel and allow them to dry.

**5.** When dry, reassemble the wine box.

**6.** Pour Blue Thunder and Zia on your palette, but don't mix them.

**7.** Take a flat brush and start painting vertical stripes of Blue Thunder and Zia from the top of the box letting some of the mahogany show through. The vertical stripes do not have to be perfectly straight.

**8.** Before it's completely dry, mist with water lightly to make the colors "melt."

**9.** Mix 2 parts Zeus to 1 part water in a small spray bottle.

10. Spray Zeus on the wine box, concentrating on the upper portion of the box. Mist Zeus here and there, concentrating on the upper portion of the piece with a lighter mist on the lower portion of the wine box.

## PRO TIPS

- Be sloppy and apply liberally.
- Don't be afraid to let some of the mahogany color peek through when wet distressing with your spray bottle of water.

11. Mist lightly with water to expose more mahogany, if you wish, and to melt the gold a bit.

12. Apply Zeus to your gloved fingers and flick small amounts, concentrating on the top and very little on the button. If the flicks turn out too big, mist lightly with water.

13. Allow it to dry before moving on to stenciling and sealing.

## Stenciling and Sealing

1. In a resealable container, mix 2 parts Athena to 1 part Midnight's Blackness. This makes a bronze-black color. Mix 1 oz. of the black-bronze custom color with three spoonfuls of PiNCH Powder. Stir well, put the lid on, and allow it to develop for 20 minutes. Once developed, stir again to create a fluffy, smooth paste.

2. Lightly apply the screen stencil anywhere on the box. Apply a small amount of the developed PiNCH Powder with a scraper—a business card will work—over the top of the screen stencil. Listen for a sound like a record scratching. Cover the area of the stencil, being careful not to go out of the area of the stencil. Apply the screen stencil lightly to your dry surface and "scrape on" your stencil paste onto the stencil surface. Use a minimal amount. There's no need to cake it on.

3. Peel off the screen stencil and repeat in other areas if desired. Depending on your preference, after the design is dry use a sanding block and sand the stencil lightly to create a distressed look. Do not sand if you want a bright image.

4. Using Zeus, splatter a bit more here and there, over and around the finished stencils.

5. Seal with SPiT SHiNE wax or the oil-based top-coat of your choice.

6. If seal sealing with SPiT SHiNE wax, you can make DiY gilding wax by mixing a few drops of Zeus (or any METALLiC) into some wax.

7. From here, you can add a golden glisten to all corners and high ridges by applying the golden wax with your brush only hitting the raised areas of the wood trim.

8. Allow your topcoat to cure and it's ready to go!

# CHAPTER TWELVE

# Redesign with the Change of Time

Throughout this book, my SPiT FAMiLY and I have shown you some of our favorite techniques with which we have great success and enjoy doing. But one thing you will see that I've repeated throughout the book is to never judge anything by its color, but instead by its bones. Having good, strong bones means it's going to be durable and ready for an afterlife if your taste in style changes. You can always keep up with the latest trends by putting on a new outfit—when you have a piece with good bones.

In this final project, I'm going to take you on a journey of this little jewelry box that started out copper and how I gave it three different looks using three different techniques. I've got to say that my Peek-a-Boo whitewash style was my favorite, but I'm eagerly awaiting to hear what your favorite was, in one of our community groups.

# Multi-Finish Jewelry Box

# Version #1: Carnival Blending and Raised Stenciling

## What you'll need

- Unicorn SPiT colors: Phoenix Fire, Zia, Lemon Kiss, Purple Hill Majesty, and Blue Thunder
- Concept color: Zeus
- Sturdy Polyethylene stencil large enough to cover the drawers
- FAMOWOOD water-based wood filler
- Plastic putty knife
- Alcohol iNK color in blue (see page 13)
- Artist brushes
- Painter's tape
- Fine grit sandpaper
- Oil-based topcoat of your choice

Carnival Blending, a tropical, exciting, vibrant style, has always been a showstopper. My friend Lauren Chapman was the first to introduce this multicolored blending style, and it was even replicated by a famous DiYer, Mark Montano. You can do this on pieces big and small and on any substrate from plastic to wood to concrete. These colors make me think of Carnival in Brazil with the dancers wearing big feathers on their heads and their multicolor sparkly outfits. It's as exciting to create this look as it is for everyone who sees it.

# Directions for drawers

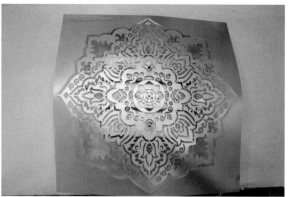

1. I found this little wood jewelry box and it looked as though it was spray-painted copper. This worked great for me because I like to wet-distress and have a metallic base exposed.

2. Remove any hardware, then stack the drawers face-side up in the same order as they belong in the box. Center your stencil over the top.

3. Use your putty knife to spread the wood filler thickly over the stencil, covering the drawer fronts entirely.

4. Slowly peel off the stencil to reveal the raised pattern that is now on your drawers. Separate the drawers and use the putty knife to remove the excess hanging off the drawer edges. Allow it to dry, which can take less than an hour.

5. Use sandpaper to lightly buff the dry design, smooth any edges, or knock down any overly large lumps.

**6.** Now that the stencil is free of lumps and ready to stain, stack them in order and secure them using painter's tape.

**7.** Coat the entire surface with undiluted Zia, leaving the center blank.

**8.** Color the center with Phoenix Fire, then color the ring around the center medallion with Lemon Kiss. At this point, it looks a little messy, but don't give up hope. On the outer ring, over the Zia, dry brush Purple Hill Majesty to just the raised areas. Allow it to dry and give it a quick shot of spray sealant.

**9.** It's time to bring this colorful mess together. While using the hair dryer, you're going to dry and color at the same time. Simply go over the muddied areas with Zia, allowing as much or as little of the Lemon Kiss and Phoenix Fire to peek through.

**10.** This is a good chance for you to touch up the Purple Hill Majesty dry brushing that you may have covered while adding more Zia.

## PRO TIP

· To make your colors more prominent and vibrant, you can do the Purple Hill Majesty and Zia first on the raised stencil, and then seal. Then add the Phoenix Fire and Lemon Kiss. This will keep the colors from muddying and will give you an additional layer of durability.

12. You can stipple your brush with Zia and go over the Phoenix Fire again. This color layering is fun and creates a lot of depth and interest. You will get tones of red and green because of the way the colors blend together.

11. Now add a little dry brushing to bring the Phoenix Fire and the Lemon Kiss back to vibrancy and out of muddiness.

## Directions for the body of the box

1. Brush on Zia with a dampened brush. Allow the colors to cling to the spray-painted surface creating a lace-like design. Let it dry.

2. After Zia is dry, apply Purple Hill Majesty with a sopping wet brush at the top of the upper side, pulling down three-quarters of the way down, and mist with water. Misting with water will blend the colors, naturally exposing some of the copper surface.

**3.** You can keep adding colors, including Lemon Kiss, misting in between to create this color palette that you see. Don't add Phoenix Fire, as it will muddy your colors. After it's dry, you can seal it. To add more interest, try the next step.

**4.** Drip your blue DiY Alcohol iNK from the top, allowing it to cascade to the bottom. Add a few drops of purple DiY Alcohol iNK as well.

**6.** Seal with your favorite oil-based topcoat. I chose to seal it with one light coat of SPiT SHiNE Wax as I wanted it to have a semi-protective finish. Replace your hardware.

**5.** You can either take a damp cloth and wipe away the color to expose the copper or you can add little punches of Phoenix Fire here and there on the piece. You can paint the top one solid color to keep the drawers the focal point.

# Version #2: Peek-a-Boo Whitewash

One of my favorite things about Unicorn SPiT is its vibrant colors. So, the last thing I wanted to do was color it all white. But, I knew I had to show you how to whitewash. But it didn't mean that I couldn't put my own spin on it. I absolutely love how I was able to allow little bits of the color to peek out of its white blanket creating a white, opal-like effect. The hint of color that I allowed to shine through was a little glimpse of the Carnival life the jewelry box had before.

## What you'll need

- Unicorn SPiT color: White Ning
- Artist brush
- Hair dryer
- Damp shop cloth
- Clear satin spray topcoat

# Directions

1. Now, it's time to mute your bold colors, but you're still going to get a peek-a-boo effect. If you want full coverage in white, you will have to be sure that your piece is completely sealed. I only had one thin coat of wax on this.

2. Apply a liberal amount of White Ning to your brush.

## PRO TIP

- One coat of wax is not strong enough to hold back Unicorn SPiT's strong pigmentation.

3. Brush White Ning all over the stencil, making sure the color is thick in all of the crevices.

4. Brush the White Ning on the sides and top. You will see a hue of the color underneath start to bleed into the white immediately since it wasn't sealed all that great before. Allow this to dry.

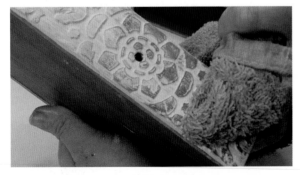

5. Remove drawers and use a damp cloth to wipe away the tops of the raised stencil to expose the color underneath as much or as little as you like.

6. After it's dry, feel free to seal with your preferred oil-based topcoat. You're going to love how this twist on whitewash becomes colorful.

# Version #3: Traditional with a Twist

There may come a time, or it could be your taste now, that you want to bring in the earth tones of brown. It's a good way to ground a piece and merge it into your current decor. Of course, I couldn't completely cover the entire piece in brown, so I decided to go with two tones. Had this been a nice, solid wood piece, I probably would have stripped the frame down to its bare wood and stained brown, leaving the drawers alone. But since it wasn't sandable wood, I created a fresh new surface using my liquid-wood canvas concoction. I gave it a look of wood by staining it a traditional warm, chestnut brown. And if I wanted to, in its next life, I would go back to the Carnival because I love it. Nothing is stopping you from continuing the evolution of designs on your pieces that have good bones.

## What you'll need

- Unicorn SPiT color: SQUiRREL
- Liquid wood canvas concoction
- Jumbo artist brush
- Spray bottle of water
- Oil based top coat of your choice

267

# Directions

1. Remove the drawers and apply the liquid-wood canvas concoction over the entire body of the box.

2. Use 220-grit sandpaper or higher to smooth any bumps or lumps in the dried liquid wood canvas concoction.

3. Water down a little bit of SQUiRREL on your palette until you get the strength of the chestnut color you desire.

4. Apply your diluted SQUiRREL onto the surface following the same brushstrokes that you used to apply the liquid-wood canvas.

5. If you like the brushstrokes, you can seal or do additional coats of SQUiRREL for a more solid color.

6. After the body is fully sealed, pop your drawers back in and now you have a traditional look with a spin.

# Conclusion: A Few Thoughts

My biggest passion now is formulating new colors, creating new art mediums, and teaching others how to use Unicorn SPiT. I didn't take chemistry in high school, but while doing these projects, the uneducated chemist in me was able to formulate new ways to use Unicorn SPiT and replace it with a multitude of art mediums like alcohol ink and translucent glass tint.

Unicorn SPiT is the medium for curious artists because it allows you to try all different types of painting techniques without the expense of having to buy all types of painting mediums. With Unicorn SPiT and a few clear catalysts, you can have the whole art-medium aisle of an arts-and-crafts store at your fingertips. Such a great space saver too!

Once you get bitten by the Unicorn SPiT bug, everyday things will become your canvas. These are just some of the basic ways that I have found to use Unicorn SPiT, but at this time, we have more than 60,000 members of a group who are discovering new ways to use Unicorn SPiT every day. The projects in this book are limited to just me and a few of my SPiT FAMiLY, but it's not limited to what you can create or DiSCOVER.

## Join Us

Reaching the end of this book doesn't mean I'm going to leave you. Instead, I want to welcome you to our online support forum that is populated with tens of thousands of crafters, woodworkers, and artists of all levels. If you discover something new, reach out to us on our Facebook group and let us know. Our group is here for community support and to help each other discover deep-seated innovations that are in every one of us. You might even make a few like-minded friends! I hope you will become part of our Unicorn SPiT FAMiLY and enjoy endless years of joyful, artistic comradery.

**For more directions, techniques, inspiration, camaraderie, or just to ask a question, join our FREE online forum at:**
bit.ly/UnicornSPiTFAMiLY

**To see projects in action, visit our YouTube channel at:**
https://www.youtube.com/c/UnicornSPiT/videos

# Meet Michelle's SPiT FAMiLY

**Pam Atteberry**, based in the Atchison, Kansas, area, has loved crafting from a young age. Her various arts and crafts projects range from drawing to hand sewing to painting and more. Pam discovered UNiCORN SPiT from a social media post a few years ago and was absolutely hooked. She was interested in learning more about how to use this product and after learning that Michelle Nicole wasn't too far from her, she made many trips to the workshop. She found a new love for this product and became great friends with Michelle. Pam loves to use Unicorn SPiT on furniture, cloth, and paper projects, to name a few. She uses it for watercoloring, stenciling, blending, and so many other things. Pam has created her own business named Glitter and Rust Creations, where she displays the many different items she creates. She lives with her husband, Mike, and their four dogs and has two children and five grandchildren. **bit.ly/GlitterAndRust**

**Cindi Carpenter** was born and raised in Southern California. She was one of the original Unicorn SPiT retailers and for as long as she can remember, she has made art. As a credited artist, she has had a few of her pieces published and has won a couple of art contests. She has also sold paintings and furniture finished with Unicorn SPiT. She has taught many classes on the use of Unicorn SPiT on a wide variety of mediums such as glass, canvas, wood signs, and more. One of her regular classes was for seniors at a senior center in her hometown. She says that there is nothing more gratifying than to create with your hands and see the end results. Art is a way of relaxing your mind and body. You can check out some of her workon Facebook at Sweet SPiTUNIAS and also DIY with the Sweet SPiTUNiAS Sisters, **bit.ly/SweetSPiTUNiAS**.

**Kimberly Cook**, based in the Cincinnati, Ohio, area, began as a self-taught furniture artist in 2015. Working with several different types of media on a variety of substrates, she discovered Unicorn SPiT through social media in early 2016. Excited to use SPiT on her furniture, her first projects were a variety of tables and desktops. From there she experimented by using Unicorn SPiT on other types of surfaces; one of her favorites has been using Unicorn SPiT on fabric lampshades. Currently she works primarily with inks and resin on a variety of surfaces. She also enjoys looking for new ways to use products to add life and interest to her projects. You can find her at **bit.ly/thirteenchairs**.

**Avera Cosplay** is a cosplayer and costume/prop maker. Cosplay is performance art, where individuals dress up in costumes to represent a certain character. For the past four years, she has been making costumes from scratch, bringing to life characters from video games like *Overwatch* and *World of Warcraft*. She also loves to take popular characters and put a new spin on them, like Armored Maleficent, Jedi Cinderella, and Playboy Bunny Belle. Cosplay is a family affair for Avera. Along with her husband, their 15-year-old son, and their 11-month-old daughter, they all get into the fun. They compete in craftsmanship competitions and have won awards at many comic conventions such as Dragon Con. By day, she is a director of media buying for a software company, but pours every extra second into her craft, growing and helping others. Her motto is: "Everyone starts somewhere, and no one is where they want to be yet. Enjoy the ride and help each other along the way!' **bit.ly/AveraCosplay**

**Stephanie Keene** lives in Connecticut. Unicorn SPiT was Stephanie's gateway to becoming an artist. She specializes in clocks, ornaments, and wall art, and also teaches Unicorn SPiT classes. She is currently working on a memoir about creativity and the transformational power of making art. She can be found online at **bit.ly/KeenecraftCreations**.

**Holly McAnlis** lives in South Dakota with her two daughters. She met her late husband during high school, in a small town in Southern Nevada called Boulder City. They were married for 42 years. After relocating in 2012, she began playing around with graphite art. She never took formal art classes and learned on her own. That same year, she became interested in wood-stain art on furniture. She began with the same monochromatic type of art until she found Michelle and Unicorn SPiT. She was hooked by the colors she had created and loved that she could control the vibrancy of her art with this new medium. She has been using Unicorn SPiT for over five years now and feels that she has mastered her style of incorporating these stains into her art. She has succeeded in growing a good following on Facebook with Holly's Hobbies 10x page.
**bit.ly/HollysHobbies**

**Karla Morris**, along with many others, discovered "SPiT" on social media. She began following Michelle Nicole on YouTube, not realizing that this bubbly, down-to-earth artist would soon become not only an inspiration but a dear friend as well. It turned out that Michelle's studio was only an hour away from Karla's small town outside of Kansas City, Missouri. She and her husband have two grown children and serve as live-in staff to three incredibly spoiled felines. Karla enjoys living in the quiet town where she can work on projects on the wraparound front porch of her two-story house that was built in 1910. This activity inspired the name of her business "Front Porch SPiTTiN.'"

**Regina (Kay) Richardson** is a self-taught artist whose creative journey has led her through decorative painting and landscape painting certifications to painting her own designs. She finds her inspiration in nature, old architecture, and travel. She discovered there is no better way to truly appreciate a beautiful locale than painting it on location. Florida provides a wide array of interesting locations to paint and a long-term vacation stop for Regina, her husband, Brian, and her studio manager, Xiu the cat.
**bit.ly/GypzPallet**

**Susi Schuele** Step into Susi's home and you see her beautiful works adorning its walls at every turn. A native of Illinois, when the opportunity presented itself after retirement, Susi decided to listen to the artist inside her that had been there since childhood. She brings a little more of her soul into each of her paintings by titling them with song. She enjoys the transformation of a piece of wood from simple, timeless and organic to vibrant, colorful, and alive via its natural grain and Unicorn SPiT.
**bit.ly/SecondTouchArt**

**Haley Sellmeyer** is a 13-year-old professional artist from the Kansas City area who loves to paint and create art. Haley's been painting and creating different types of art since she was 1 year old. Born two months premature, her mother was trying to find things to stimulate her brain and art happened to be one of those things. Haley has participated in over 100 art exhibitions, including juried art shows, gallery shows, and charity events, and has won numerous awards for her art. She has also been featured on several live radio segments, television news channels, and in several newspapers in and around the Kansas City area. **bit.ly/HaleyArtwork**

**Isaac Stark** is on the autism spectrum and has two rare medical conditions. As a result, the 13-year-old has sensory issues that hinder him from being able to do many of the things we take for granted in everyday life. Isaac has struggled to even wash his hands, because the sensation of the water bothers him. Throughout the years he has attended occupational therapy focused on motor skills. Unfortunately, this offered very little to help with his sensory issues.

His artist mother, Trish, decided to try using art to help him with his tactile sensory issues. In the beginning it was difficult for him. He struggled to focus on anything other than the sensations he felt on his hands. However, Isaac soon discovered a love for creating beautiful things. Isaac continues to do art weekly to grow as an artist and overcome his sensory issues. Isaac now has a YouTube channel, where he provides instructions on simple art projects others can do to have fun and, hopefully, help someone else with sensory issues. The Starks discovered Unicorn SPiT Gel Stain through a paint-pouring Facebook group. It was important that the products used during Isaac's art sessions were easy to wash off. This is one of the main reasons they decided to give it a try. **bit.ly/IsaacsArtStudio**

**Terri Viner-Billett** has been crafting for many years using a variety of mediums. Although she has chronic health issues, she finds it therapeutic to keep busy. She restores furniture and ceramics as well as upcycles random objects into usable beautiful home decor. Her handcrafted garden ornaments are available through Facebook, Instagram, and at her partner's garden center in Leicestershire, England. **bit.ly/TerriVinerBillet**

# Resources

Featured interior topcoats, decoupage, strippers, brushes, Unicorn SPiT, ARTiSTiC ViVATiONS, Concept Colors, Paper Clay, PiNCH Powder, SPiT SHiNE, Hemp Sealing Salve, Fabric Fuse, FAMOWOOD Wood Filler, and FAMOWOOD Glaze Coat

> www.MichelleNicoles.com
> Discount Code: SPiTBOOK for 10 percent off

Unicorn SPiT, E6000 Plus Glue, E6000 Fabri-Fuse, E6000 Spray Adhesive, and FAMOWOOD Glaze Coat and Famowood Wood Filler

> Eclectic Products
> www.eclecticproducts.com

Wood Surfaces, wood burner, and tissue boxes

> www.WalnutHollow.com

String art blanks, canvases, and box wine caddies

> www.TechnicolorSneekers.com
> **Discount Code:** UnicornSPiT

Decorative Transfers and Silicone Moulds

> bit.ly/Transfers-Molds

Custom Screen Stencil Maker

> bit.ly/ScreenStencilMaker
> **Discount code:** UnicornSPiT

Live Edge Wood

> GotBarnWood.com

Sola Wood Flowers

> bit.ly/SolaWoodFlowers
> **Discount Code:** UnicornSPiT

Be sure to visit your local Goodwill, Salvation Army, and other charity thrift shops for fabulous secondhand treasure hunting. Reduce, Reuse, Recycle and turn it into ART!

# Acknowledgments

The world is a beautiful place thanks to people who encourage, help, and teach others. I enjoy basking in all of the glory the world has to offer and am never afraid to request a special dose of a friend's talent.

Through the years of living in Kansas, I have made quite a few friends. Most have opposing hobbies, but we always have cocktails and dancing in common.

As motherhood took grasp of my life and the disco balls faded, I found myself enjoying time spent with my son's best friend's mom, Amanda. Amanda likes to read, play with photography, and draw. We obviously have a lot in common other than reading, lol! I knew Amanda would be the perfect copilot for all the projects I needed to create for the book. She did an amazing job keeping me on task, taking photos, and making rhyme out of my reason. I couldn't have had better support than what Amanda blessed this book with. She is full of hidden talents and is a digital art fairy with her photography and video-editing abilities. She's like magic!

Editing is a nightmare. Putting words together in text and editing down my ramblings is no small obstacle. It is like a calculated fight. I'm sure of it. It has to be the worst part. At least for me, it was just simply unbearable. I quit many times. I knew I needed a tough, smart, and articulate badass that would grab me by my ear if they had to, so I called on my friend, Lisa Kanarek. Lisa has strong-armed me through this book. She dedicated her muscles and brains to squeeze every last drop of creativity from my brain and help me transform this book into a comprehensible masterpiece. Without her, I think this book would have just been a bunch of goofy made-up words (that you'd get eventually) to describe everything including thoughts three steps ago. See what I mean? Thank you, Lisa. You helped me and the readers make sense of my whimsical madness.

Children also feed my creativity with their innocence and the willingness to see things in a new light. Haley Sellmeyer and Issac Stark have shown me things I never knew possible. Haley created a way to use my stencil powder to thicken SPiT and create oil painting-like art that solves oil painting problems. She gave us all the ability to act like Bob Ross and paint "happy little trees" just like him, without harsh chemicals. She opened my eyes to a whole new way to paint that I just simply forgot about trying.

Issac, despite his conditions, has shown that with wellness, support, joy, and love in your heart, you can overcome things you thought you couldn't; that disabilities can turn into unique abilities that radiate healing!

Terri Viner-Billett overcomes her health issues and raises her spirits by creating beautiful art through casting plaster and cement. That is something for which I just don't have the knowledge or patience. She was the perfect person to call upon to share her talents. I'm so happy Terri took the time to create a beautiful piece of art just to teach us.

Holly McAnlis is a dear soul, too. She endlessly helps others in our Facebook Q&A group. She answers questions and encourages every newbie and pro alike. With the recent passing of her husband, creating art and helping others is her form of self-love therapy. Her blooming tabletops give me joy knowing they are a direct reflection of her endlessly blooming heart. Thank you, Holly, for being such a magnificent element in our Unicorn SPiT world.

Kimberly Cook has always made a splash in our blessing of unicorns. You may not hear much from her in our Q&A, but she is always there to wow us with her bold new ideas. She is always up for a challenge and ready to impress. I'm honored to have you contribute to our SPiT book with your gorgeous colorful creations.

Avery Cosplay (Nicole Wilcox), you, my dear, are exciting and full of imagination. There was no one better to take Unicorn SPiT to the furthest edges from pretend to reality. Your unique spin on bringing color to the comic world is sure to inspire for generations to come! Thank you for enchanting this book with your creation.

One-stroke painting and acrylic painting is not something I should teach anyone about; I don't get to play with it enough to feel confident teaching others. So I sought out my friend Regina Richardson—whom I call Kay. Regina supported me while I sought instruction on acrylic-style paintings, then she turned around and found she could do everything with SPiT! I couldn't believe it! She made things feel secure for me in a world where others gave me the cold shoulder because I didn't use the same tools. Thank you, Kay, for embracing my concepts and showing everyone through your gorgeous art that SPiT is an important medium to add to your artist's arsenal. You showed them and I thank you for it!

Susi Schuele, I don't even know where to begin. As one of the very first to believe in me before I even knew how to use PayPal, you have offered your talents to grow my dream. You created our very first website, made my first business card, designed the first labels, and armed me with the digital knowledge I needed to dazzle the world with a new art medium. Along the way, you released the fine artist that has been waiting for her wings. You have been a friend and advisor for everything from life to business. I think we are soul sisters, and it was an honor to walk down the aisle in your wedding dress. I love you so! Beth, you too. Don't say I didn't mention you.

Pam Atteberry and Karla Morris, thank you for comforting me while I had breakdowns and letdowns through the years. Thank you, also, for celebrating with me through all the good times, too! Having you girls contribute to the book was really for me to relish in our friendship and encapsulate it for all of time. You gals are my good, best girlfriends and keep me happy. Thank you for always being there for me no matter what.

Speaking of having our backs, Theresa Waugh from Eclectic Products is my Fairy Godmother. This lady picked me up when I was brewing SPiT in a spaghetti pot and took my ideas and concepts around the world. She didn't know me from Adam but knew there was something special about Unicorn SPiT. She took a leap of faith and embraced me. Thank you, Theresa, for always knowing what's best and leading our brand into becoming the best art medium in the whole world. You gave me more than glass slippers—you gave my invention and confidence wings!

I may have never listed the folks named above if it wasn't for a magical gathering of random strangers who came into my life because of color on social media. Michelle Kline, Laurie Crews, Barb Minutello, Evey Flores, Andrew Spitznagle, Michelle Austin, Marlies Soltys, Brenda Jones, Pat German-Small, Mary Klier, Carol Kenworthy, Lisa Roark, and many, many others...so many this paragraph would take a whole page. These folks reached out, started a calling, banded together, and made an unspoken

Michelle and Unicorn pact. They all support and reinforce my colorful concepts endlessly. Since the very beginning, too. Ups and downs, lefts and rights, they have never faltered. They have been tried and true. Thank you for always walking alongside me even when I mess up.

As y'all know, I have a big brother, Tony. He taught me how to tie my shoes and ride a bike. He is a dork, but he's sharp. He and I make a good team because he listens to my ideas and then makes them even cooler. In the long run, I have to acknowledge our partnership in idea sorcery is epic. So thanks, Tony, for showing me how to tie my shoes and how to crash gracefully.

My boys definitely need to be acknowledged. Johnny, Joshua, and Jamey, the "Three J's," have helped me every step of the way. From putting labels on the bottles to finger-combing my hair when they see I'm stressed. These boys have loved and believed in me endlessly. They always help hunt treasures, move big things, clean up, and never let me down. I couldn't have asked for better sons.

They are all perfectly imperfect with love as their greatest perfection.

Last, but not least, I want to thank my husband, Don Dean Day. He's not only super handsome and tough as nails, but he's soft, supportive, and affectionate as a teddy bear. Curling up with him every night is my safe place, my home, and my heaven on earth. Thank you for being my protector and cuddle bug who also believes in me.

Without the experiences and support from my peers and team at Ultimate Software, this book would not exist. You have given me the opportunity to lead a great group of individuals—to be a leader of great leaders is a blessed place to be. Thank you to Chad, Dan, Dave, Gretchen, JC, Laura, Patrick, Scott, and Susan.

Having an idea and turning it into a book is as hard as it sounds. The experience is both internally challenging and rewarding. I especially want to thank the individuals that helped make this happen. Complete thanks to Joanie, Randy Walton, Patrick O'Neill, Barbara Boyd, Carol Raphael, and Dan Bernitt.

# About the Author

**Michelle Nicole** is a self-taught artist with a passion for color, design, and art therapy. Whether she's transforming an outdated piece of furniture into a sleek, stylish piece, or formulating new colors to add to her popular line of Unicorn SPiT products, her creative mind is always in motion. In addition to discovering new ways to use her ingenious product, Michelle enjoys teaching others how to "let your creative juices flow." The videos she posts online for tens of thousands of followers are informative and entertaining. No item, surface, or piece of clothing is off limits. As Michelle says, "You can SPiT that!"